ELVIRA CRAIG

Yes, He is Enough

End Times Harvest Publications Ministries
Publishers since 1995

Yes, He Is Enough

All Scripture quotes in this book are taken from the King James Version, Holy Bible.

End Times Harvest Publication Ministries
Subsidiary of Bible Teaching Fellowship Ministries

Library of Congress Cataloging-in Publication Data
Craig, Elvira
Yes, He Is Enough
ISBN 978-1-8911680-39-0 (eBook)

Printed in United States of America

Special Thanks

The wonderment continues... The love and support given so freely to me. Always and forever, my dear, Carlton.

I am so amazed and delighted by all the beautiful array of ladies in my life. Like a lovely bouquet of flowers, these remarkable ladies fill my life with brilliant colors of strength, laughter, hope, joy, and sisterhood. Thank you, ladies. You truly have provided me with plenty of writing material-smile.

Table of Contents

Chapter One
The Reunion

"Yes, yes, Myra, this is the day! I am so glad I am off work and on vacation. Myra, my goodness, this year Robert has been such a taskmaster. Girl, he was still trying to give me work as I was leaving out the door today." Liz pranced about the room holding her new bright yellow bathing suit against herself. "Girl!" She screamed into the phone, "I am on vacation for two long weeks! Do you hear me, Myra? I am on vacation."

"Yes, girl, I hear you, so you can stop yelling on this phone."

"Ah, Myra, do not be a hater. I understand you cannot celebrate yet because you have two more days of work."

Myra glanced down at the calendar on her desk, "Yes, you, are right, Liz, but my bags are packed. As soon as I am off work I am heading straight to the airport to sunny California. I will live on the beach for a week."

"Yeah, Myra, count me in too."

"Oh, girl, what am I thinking about? I need to get off this phone with you and call Sydney before I leave this house to see if she needs me to do anything before, I fly out in the morning."

"Yes, get off the phone with me because you are making a sister want to call off work."

"Okay, Myra, you better not even think about it. You are already on shaky ground," laughed Liz. "Then, girl, you will be crying about being on a permanent vacation."

"Just be quiet, Liz. I am not going to call off work. By the way, what time does your flight leave in the morning?"
"Seven a.m."
"What! seven a.m.!" screamed Myra! "Why so early?"
"Myra, what do you mean why so early? Because I want to spend every second on vacation."
Myra sighed. "Well, okay. I will see you on Friday."
"Friday? Myra. I thought you were flying in on Thursday so you can be at Taylor's birthday party?"
"What? Birthday party! Girl, no! When I arrive in Cali I am on vacation, and I am not going to be bothered with anybody's kids. I am on vacation. I am sick of kids. Liz, I am so glad to be getting away from my sister's bad kids."
"Okay, Myra. I have told you to stop calling those kids bad."
"No, Liz, I am calling them what they are, just bad! Last Saturday my three-year-old niece decided to plug my toilet with her teddy bear."
"Wait a minute, Myra didn't you have the kids last weekend while your sister and her husband went out of town?"

"Well, yes…but what does that got to do with anything? That is why I can say that they are bad. Do you know how much plumbers cost these days? That little big-eyed brat cost me a pair of Jimmy Choo's."

"What! That much, girl? Okay, Myra, are we talking about real Jimmy Choo's?"

"Well, the knock-offs, but do not tell anyone. Anyway, that is beside the point. Her little butt cost me money I did not have.

So, Liz, when I get to Cali, I do not want to see, hear or smell any bratty kids."

"Okay," laughed Liz, "I will see you on Friday at the beach house."

"Yes, you will, girlfriend. By the way, is Sydney picking you up from the airport or are you renting a car? Because you know the traffic getting from the airport is the worst."

"Oh, yes, you are right," laughed Liz. Yes, girl, let me go right now. I got to called Sydney, and find out."

"Okay, bye. I will talk to you when I get to Cali."

Liz excitedly dialed Sydney's number.

Sydney answered with a sleepy raspy voice, "Hello?"

"Sydney? Sydney? This is Liz. Did I wake you?" Sydney, with an airless voice, slowly answers.

"Oh, no, Liz, you didn't wake me."

"Girl, I am so sorry. I forgot about our time zone differences. Were you asleep?" Sydney sobbed as she answered.

"No, Liz, I am up. Sydney, girl, what in the world is wrong? Are your kids okay?" Sydney paused.

"Sydney, Sydney, come on, tell me what's going on."

"I hate Clarence!" Liz releases a deep breath.

"Okay, Sydney, I am not trying to be funny, but that is not a new revelation. You are always saying you hate Clarence. But why has it brought you to tears?"

"Liz, you know, I have been waiting all year for our reunion week."

"Yes, Sydney."

"Well, sadly to say, I may not be able to join you guys this week."
"Okay, Sydney what are you talking about? I just talked to you last night. What could have possibly happened overnight?"
"Clarence will not take his kids."
"What!" shouted Liz! "What do you mean Clarence will not take his kids? They are his kids. Last week when we talked, everything was fine. What has happened? You didn't tell him you were going to the beach house with us, did you?"
"No, no, I didn't tell him. Unfortunately, Daniel did."

"What! Do you mean Daniel, your little brother, told him? What on earth would possess him to tell Clarence about our beach trip? Sydney, I am confused. Does not Daniel equally dislike Clarence? So why did he tell him?"

"Well, Liz, Daniel claimed it was an accident. He did not know that Clarence did not know. I asked Daniel to pick up all of you from the airport in the morning and I was going to wait here for Clarence to get the kids. Well, last night Daniel said he ran into Clarence at the gym. You know Clarence being so nosy he started asking Daniel a lot of questions, who I was seeing and stuff. Daniel should have told Clarence what I am doing was none of his business. Instead, he did not want Clarence to think I did not have a life. So Daniel told him I had plans to see someone this week while the kids were with him. Well, Clarence, the monster, is at it again, trying to stop me from having a life without him. Let me tell you what this low life of a man did. He called me on the phone and cussed me out and said he was not picking up his kids so I could go have a freak week with another man. Now, can you believe that? Yeah, right, I am having a freak week with another man. Did this crazy man forget why we divorced? Liz, he has conveniently forgotten that it was him that brought all kinds of freaks into our marriage. Now he wants to know what I am doing. I have not had a date in two years. I got so mad that I called Daniel and asked him what he was thinking to tell Clarence anything about what I was doing. Daniel felt so bad that he called Clarence and told him the truth. But Clarence did not believe him. And he still will not change his pig-headed mind and take his kids this week even after Daniel told him the truth." Sydney cried uncontrollably.

"Liz, I work so hard taking care of my kids. I truly love them. But am I a bad mom for looking forward to this time away? I hate Clarence. I hate that he is the father of my kids. They deserve a much better father. My kids are such great kids. I hate that they have such a monster like Clarence for a dad."

"Sydney, my God, it will be all right."

"No, it will not be all right, Liz!" screamed Sydney.

"And now, now, I have the painful job of telling my kids. How do I explain it to them? They have been excited for months about going to spend a whole week with their dad. I am so mad, I am so mad. I just hate him for doing this to my kids, all because he wanted to stick it to me. What about his kids? Why do not men understand they hurt their kids when they play these stupid games? Remember, Liz, I told you about my girlfriend Rita who lives here. She is going through the same ridiculous stuff. She hates her kids' dad too. Liz, I know what you are going to say, but I think that even Jesus hates what Clarence is doing to my kids, does not he? I hate Clarence," cried Sydney. "And to top it off, Clarence is acting like we are one big happy family. Well, we are not! I hate Clarence!"

Sydney, cried quietly. "Liz, you just do not understand. It is just terrible having Clarence as their dad. It is the worst thing I ever did. I hate that I ever married Clarence, and I hate he is the father of my children."

"Sydney, I am so sorry about what has happened. Come on, let us just give this situation and yourself to God. I know it is overwhelming and yes, I know I do not fully understand, but Jesus does. Sydney, I do know how it feels to be overwhelmed by circumstances. That's why I know your only answer is to give this situation and yourself to Christ."

Sydney paused and whispered, "I know. I know. Perhaps God is just angry at me, or maybe this is some kind of punishment because I stopped going to church. Sydney deeply sighed, "Girl, I do not know. I am not sure about anything anymore, Liz. I am so overwhelmed, and I am tired of everything being on me. I love my kids, but it is something when you have to handle everything and deal with a crazy baby daddy too." Sydney cried. "Liz, it's too much it is just simply too much."

"Sydney, trust me when I tell you that God is not angry with you, and He is definitely not punishing you. Sydney, just take a deep breath and listen to me for just a few minutes. Sydney, good or bad, our lives are driven by the choices we make. I am not trying to put you down. So please hear my heart out. My point is when we make choices, good or bad, we have to live with the consequences of our choices. Which hopefully we can change things in our life by making better choices leading to better outcomes. So yes, being a single parent is overwhelming, and especially when you have to deal with your kids' dad who is so challenging. But there is hope. Make the choice by bringing all of this stuff to God. Only He can give to you the peace and assurance you need and want. Sydney, girl, I am so sorry about what is happening, especially to your kids. It does not matter how painful something is. Right now, just make the choice to give it to Christ. And then do not worry about it. Just bring the kids with you this week. It will be okay. Everyone will understand."

Sydney paused. "Liz, everyone? Everyone will understand? No, no, not everyone will, right, Liz?"

"Well, yeah, okay, Liz responded. "I know you are talking about Myra. Girl, do not be concern with Myra. She will be just fine."

"Well, I am not sure about bringing them, Liz. This week was about us getting away and spending time catching up with one another. It has been ten years since we were all together. Not since our college days. My, my, somebody is getting old."

"Old, who are you calling old, Sydney? We are the same age. Wow, Sydney, where has the time gone?"

"Well, I know my time has been spent being a single mom, which fills my entire day. No, Liz, I got to think of something else to do. It is so nice of you to say that I could bring my kids, but I will not come if I have to do that. If I do not find other arrangements, I will just give Daniel the key to Mission Impossible and all of you can go without me."

"That is it, Sydney. I could not remember what we called your grandfather's beach house. Mission Impossible. Girl, remember when we all would come down during spring break. We would say our mission is to have fun, and it will be impossible for anyone to stop us."

Sydney laughed, "Liz, I will call you back later once I get myself together."

"Okay, Sydney, but before you go, let us pray."

"No, no, Sydney interrupted. "Liz, you need to pray for Clarence so I will not kill him once I see him."

"Yes, Sydney, I will pray for Clarence, but we will also need to pray because you've got to tell your kids."

Sidney softly whispered, "Oh, yes, that's right. Yes, yes, please pray for me. I will need all the help I can get when I talk to my kids."

Chapter Two

Girlfriends Forever

Over the echo of the stewardess' announcement to board flight number 733 to California, Rebecca heard her name called out by a familiar voice. "Rebecca! Rebecca," screamed Liz. "I didn't know we were on the same flight."

"I know, I wanted to surprise you. It is so good to see you, Liz! I also wanted to come early so I can spend more time with everyone."

"My sentiments exactly. Rebecca, girl, you look so good."

"Thanks, Liz. You look fabulous yourself. Girl, it is hard to believe it has been ten years since we were all together.

"Wow, where has the time gone? I am so excited. Well, I know we got a lot of catching up to do when we all get together."

"I know, Rebecca. It has been ten years! Well, I hope we do not let another ten years pass before we meet up again. Is there anyone else on this plane,"

Liz stopped and quickly turned around as she could hear her name being screamed down the corridor.

"Liz! Liz! Wait up!"

"Who in the world? Who is screaming my name like that? Rebecca, who is that?"

"Uhm, it looks like, uh, Myra, Liz?"

"No, that is not Myra. I just talked to her, and she is not leaving until Friday. Oh, my goodness." The two women stopped and stared at each other in total unbelief.

Liz whispered, “Is that Samantha? Samantha Reed? It cannot be.”

Samantha talked with Myra on the phone as she excitedly greets Liz. “Well, how in the world are you, Liz? Do not just stand there staring come and give me a hug.”

Liz turned and mouthed the words to Rebecca.

“Who told her about our reunion?”

“Hey, Myra,” Samantha returned to her phone conversation with Myra. “I found her. I will talk to you later. Oh, no, girl, you will not guess who is here.”

“Who, girl?” asked Myra.

“That fake rich traitor, Little Mrs. Rebecca Whitman.”

“What?” Screamed Myra.

“Yes, girl, let me get off this phone. I will call you later, Myra.”

“Okay, now, do not go catching a case, Myra laughed, “because you are a lady.”

“Bye, girl.”

“Samantha, where are you going?”

“Liz, do not be funny. I am going to Mission Impossible to be with you all. Myra called me about four months ago and told me to make plans to come to Cali for the reunion. You know, Liz, we are girlfriends forever.”

“Yes, we are.” Liz spoke apprehensively as she turned and looked at Rebecca.

“Well, hello, Samantha,” Rebecca said softly.

“Hey.”

“Liz, girl, I am so excited to see you. Ten years, wow you look so good. No babies, that is the secret. Well, I am just saying you can be a homecoming queen in college, but after a couple of kids, well it, let us say it all goes south.”

Samantha slowly turned and looked at Rebecca. "Unless you are rich enough to pay to get it all fixed."

Liz looked confused. "Huh? Samantha, you were not the homecoming queen."

"Liz, girl, I know. I was not talking about me. All my stuff is real. Well, except for my hair. But everything else is 100%, or, well, at least 99% real. You know, I was going to fly in with Myra on Friday, but she told me that you were flying out today. So I changed my flight to come with you so we can catch up on good old times and hear what everyone else has been doing since college."

"Liz," whispered to Rebecca, "I will be back. I need to go to the ladies' room before we get on the plane."

"Oh, okay, Rebecca."

Samantha interjects with a snide tone, "Oh, yeah, why do not you just do that."

"Okay, Samantha, now girl, we must talk," Liz said firmly. Samantha, listen, I have been waiting all year for this week. So Samantha, let us get it all out in the air right here and right now."

Defiantly, Samantha snapped back. "Liz, Myra did not tell me that Rebecca was coming."

Liz moved closer to Samantha and leaned in. "It has been ten years. You have got to bury the hatchet. Why are you bringing up that homecoming queen and kid stuff? Girl, we are all ten years older and our college days are over. No need to open old wounds. Besides, it was not her fault and you know that. He fell in love with her, he chased her, and he wanted her. I know you know that."

"No, no, I do not know that. We were supposed to be best friends. We all made a vow that we would be girlfriends forever. She betrayed all of our trust."

"No, No, girl. What in the world are you talking about Samantha?"

"Rebecca did not betray all of our trust, "said Liz.

"She just." Liz voice trailed off as Rebecca quickly approached.

"Hey, Liz, oh, Rebecca, hey, ready to board?"

"Liz, I am glad we have seats together because I need to talk to you."

"I know, Rebecca, but let us pray first."

Rebecca calmly responded to Liz. "Yes, that's what I did when I went to the ladies' room. I knew it would also give you and Samantha time to talk. I needed time to pray especially after Samantha made remarks about me being the homecoming queen, being so rich that I had plastic surgery to look good after having my kids, which is not true. She will never believe me that I did not know about her feelings for Matthew when we were in college. Honestly, I am not going to spend this week trying to make her believe something that happened ten years ago. I am willing to have a relationship with her, but not like this. Liz, ever since we made plans to return to Mission Impossible, I have been so excited about seeing everyone. I thank God we all have each other, and we can come together because we are girlfriends forever. My concern is if Matthew finds out that she is here, he will press me to immediately come home. Liz, it is unbelievable for the first two years of our marriage she caused so much stress in our relationship."

Surprised, Liz turned to Rebecca, "My goodness, Rebecca, I did not know that. I didn't know Samantha ever contacted you after you guys got married."
"I know, I didn't tell you, Liz, because you guys were such close friends. I had to pray a lot, but the Lord blessed my heart not to grow bitter against her. Once our relationship became known, Matthew talked to me about his relationship with Samantha. He told me that they were friends and they never were intimate, nor did he ever lead her on. He was unaware of her feelings for him. Matthew said at the time, and even now he only wanted two things, God and me. He thought he and Samantha were just good friends."

"Rebecca, she knows that. Samantha told me back in the day how much she loved him. When I would question her concerning that I saw no interest in her from Matthew, she would say. 'Just wait. Matthew is not like the other guys, he is different. Matthew is a Christian. He is not going to be all over me.' But she assured me that their relationship would blossom into more as time went on. That is why she blames you. Because she thought that their relationship would have grown if you were willing to step out of the picture once you knew she loved him. Listen, girl, I have said repeatedly, 'Sam, Sam, you, know Matthew fell in love with Rebecca. Matthew chased her and he wanted her.' And she knows that. Samantha thinks you betrayed everyone by keeping your relationship a secret."

"I know, Liz, I know she does not believe me why I wanted to keep our relationship a secret. I just wanted to get to know him and pray to see if the Lord wanted me in a relationship with him. I was totally unaware of Samantha's feelings at the time."

"I know, Rebecca, and she knows it too. Samantha told me of her feelings of being in love with him, and she swore me to secrecy. I warned her then that I saw no evidence that Matthew wanted a romantic relationship with her. But to Samantha everything was a sign, until Matthew told her he was in love with you. As his friend, he confided in her his love for you. She was crushed, especially when she found out you guys had been dating for a year and he was ready to pop the question. Samantha kept it together while she was around Matthew, but soon she could not be friends with him any longer. She became unglued and angry."

"I know, Liz, I felt so sorry for everything that happened. The strange thing is that Samantha accused Matthew of knowing that she was in love with him, and she said Matthew had used their friendship just to get close to me."

"Rebecca, I tried to tell her that she was wrong, but she is still in denial."

Rebecca turned and looked at Liz with tear-filled eyes. "I truly understand Samantha's feelings of pain and rejection. You know how Reginald treated me in college. I thank God for the power of prayer. Liz, I really felt bad for her. I really did not know."

"Well, I have had enough, Rebecca, let us pray. Think about this. Perhaps this whole thing is of the Lord's doing. Rebecca shook her head in agreement. "Wow, yes, it could very well be.

Because we got both Samantha and Myra with us this week. This will be truly a Mission Impossible," laughed, Liz.
"Oh, my goodness, girl, yes, we will need prayer to be strengthened for this week. I forgot we need to pray for Sydney as well."
"Why, what is going on with Sydney?" asked Rebecca?

"Clarence is not picking up his kids for the week, and now she said she might not come. I told her to bring the kids, but I am not sure I convinced her to do so. You know she brought up Myra and how she would act."
"Liz, Myra needs to grow up. I thought she got better because does not she get her niece and nephew?"
"Yes, she does, but girl, she complains the whole time, and she always refers to them as bad."
"Bad? Liz! If I am not mistaken, they are all under the age of six."
"Yes. Well, Myra will have to get over it."
"That's the same thing I told Sydney."
"Why did Sydney ever agree to let Clarence take the kids in the first place? Didn't he do this about a year ago or so?"
"Yes, he did, Rebecca, but Sydney told me since then he had gotten better. And it was Clarence who wanted them, Sydney was going to send them to her parents for the week, but Clarence insisted on getting them, only to back out at the last minute. Now it is too late for her to arrange last minute flights to her mom, plus Taylor's birthday party is on Friday."

“Well, you are truly right, Rebecca. It is time to pray. “Yes, yes, Lord,” Liz said. “This week just got started, and I cannot believe there is already a lot going on.”

Chapter Three

Should 've & Would've

Belinda called Sydney, "Hello, Sydney."
"Hey, girl, this is Belinda."
"Belinda, Belinda, shouted Sydney, Oh, my goodness, how are you?"
"I am doing great! How are you, Sydney?"
"I am doing all right, Belinda."
"Sydney, I got your number from Liz before she got on the plane. I am flying out on Friday and needed to know what time the other crew is coming in. I also wanted to know if I needed to rent a car."
"Just like old times, Belinda is always taking care of all of us. No, I took care of it. My brother Daniel will play chauffeur this week for all of you."
"Honestly? Daniel, your little brother?"
"Well, yes, Belinda. He is not little anymore."
"Yes, you are right. Sydney, I forgot that was ten years ago. Hey, Sydney, how are your babies? Sorry I will not get there in time for Taylor's birthday party, but I got a gift for the little guy. It is too bad I will not have time to see them. You better have lots of pics this week for me to look at."
"Well, I might as well inform you. I will not be joining you ladies this week at Mission Impossible."

"What!" yelled Belinda. "What do you mean you will not be there this week? Wait, Sydney, is one of your kids sick? What in the world is going on, Sydney?"

Sydney quietly sighed, "Belinda, have you ever looked back at something and wish you should've, would've?

"Humm, yes, Sydney, I have, but do not tell me that Clarence is not picking up his kids for this week. Do not tell me, Sydney, he canceled on those kids."

"I hate that I married Clarence. I should have never married Clarence, and I would not be in this stupid position. I was so dumb. I love my kids, I really do, but what I hate most is the fact that Clarence is the father of my kids. He is a low-down monster. I have not had the heart to tell the kids yet because I want Taylor to enjoy his birthday party before breaking the news to them. They will be devastated, Belinda. This will destroy their little hearts. They already do not believe him because he has promised so many other times and did not follow through. I had a long talk with Clarence when he first requested to get the kids during spring break. I did not want him to get them because he did the same thing two years ago. But since then he has been being good about getting the kids at least one weekend a month. I warned him if he canceled, I would never let him see them again. And to think he is canceling because he thinks I am going off this week with some guy."

"What," yelled Belinda. "Why does he think that, not that it is any of his business what you do?"

"Well, Belinda, Daniel told him that as a joke."

"Sydney, what are you talking about?"

Softly Sydney, spoke. "It is a long story, Belinda, and at this moment it does not matter. I cannot join you ladies this week."

"No, no, no, stop there, Sydney. W here is your faith? Is that what you want, not to come to Mission Impossible for a week?"

"Huh, what? Belinda, where is my faith? I do not have any faith in Clarence."

"You better not have any faith in Clarence. I am talking about having faith in God. Sydney, you are acting like you do not know how to call on God."

"Listen, Belinda, I have tried. I cannot-well, I'm not-well, I'm not as strong as you."

"Sydney, I know it has been a long-time, but have you been studying the Bible?"

"Yes, yes, Belinda, it had been a long time, and no, no, I have not been studying the Bible. Listen, with the kids and work, by the time I finish with all the care and the house stuff, I just collapse into my bed. I know I should read, but Belinda, I am tired. And yes, I know. I know, Belinda, I should take the kids to church. I do not know what is wrong, but I am exhausted as a single mom."

"Sydney, I know. Being a single mom gets to be pretty challenging." Sydney quickly interrupted, "But Belinda, you've got support you've got a good man."

"Yes, you are right. Mark is a wonderful husband, but we both work and it's still challenging because we are both so tired when we get home. Yes, yes, being a single mom must be very overwhelming. But that is why we need the Lord. As mothers we have got to depend on God's Word and stay connected to the church. Sydney, if you had a church family,

you would find other single moms and other resources to help you as a single parent. Do you know there are so many promises in God's Word to strengthen parents, whether we are married or single? The Bible tells us to cast all of our cares on the Lord because he cares for us."
"Belinda, does it actually say that?"
"Yes, Sydney, it literally says that. Listen, I am going to text the Scripture to you so you can read it for yourself."
"Please do, Belinda. I'm sending it to you right now." *Casting all your care upon him; for he careth for you.1 Peter 5:7 KJV*

Sydney quietly cried on the phone. "You know, early during the day, Belinda, Liz prayed for me too. And now you call and are telling me this. I know this is the Lord calling me back, this is the Lord trying to get my attention. Belinda, I am so angry inside. I need God to help me with this rage I have towards Clarence. I have worked so hard to put my life back together since the divorce. I have tried to work things out with Clarence, but it never works out, ending the same way each time with a big conflict. I give up, Belinda. I do not know anymore what else to do. I do not know if I will ever be happy again."
"Sydney, I understand you have tried and failed, but what if I told you there is something better than happiness? It is call joy. The Bible said the joy of the Lord is our strength."
"That sounds good and all, Belinda, but I am tired."
"You are tired, Sydney, because you are doing it yourself."
"Well, okay, Belinda, let us pray."
"Sydney, before we get started you need to ask forgiveness. You need to ask forgiveness for hating Clarence."

"What! Belinda, I need to ask forgiveness for how Clarence treated me? Is that what you are saying?"
"No, Sydney, I said that you need forgiveness for how you feel about Clarence."
"Girl, did not I tell you what Clarence did to me and my kids? Why on earth would I be asking forgiveness for Clarence being a monster?"
"Again, Sydney, I asked you to ask forgiveness because of how you feel about Clarence."
"Sydney breathed deeply, "Belinda, just pray right now, because right now I cannot wrap my mind around that."
"Okay, Sydney, let us pray."
"Thank you, Belinda, for praying for me."
"You are welcome, Sydney. I need you to trust God going forward."
"Okay, I got to go and see if he is ready to go to pick up Liz and the others from the airport," said Sydney.
"Goodbye, Belinda, and thanks again."
Sydney, screamed from the kitchen, "Oh, my goodness Daniel, it is eight a.m. Are you ready?
"Has their plane landed yet," asked Daniel?
"No. Daniel. If we are 50 minutes from the airport, why would you wait to leave until their plane has landed?"
"Because a brother hates playing musical chairs at the airport. Going around and around in circles until someone comes out, I hate that, so I do not want to get there early only to get on the airport's merry-go-round."
"Silly! Just go now! Traffic on the 405 is always bad, so just leave now."

"Okay, I am leaving now."

As the ladies landed in the airport in California reached the baggage claim, "Hey, Rebecca and Samantha, could one of you guys please grab my luggage," asked Liz, "The one with the big yellow ribbons tied to the handles. I have got to go to the restroom. I held it the whole trip because I hate using those cramped restrooms on the plane."

"I will get it, Liz," said Samantha. "I am sure I am the only one used to carrying my own bags."

Liz looked back at Samantha, mouthing with her lips and signing with her hands to Samantha and cutting at her neck to cut it off.

"Okay, ugh."

Rushing to the ladies' room, Liz called Myra, "Hello Myra," I only got a few minutes. Our plane just landed, and I ran to the restroom and I only have a few minutes to talk."

"Okay, okay, yes, Liz, I already know why you are calling me."

"Girl, what were you thinking? Why would you do that? Why am I asking you anything? Listen, Myra, you know we are girlfriends forever, but if you ruin this week for me, not being your girlfriend will be the least of your problems."

"Okay, Liz, You are taking this thing way too far. All I did was invite the girl."

"Myra, you know, perfectly well, the situation between Rebecca and Samantha."

"Girl, Liz, it's been ten years. They need to get over it."

"Well, I will tell you what, Myra. While they are getting over that, you get over the fact that Sydney is bringing her kids this week.

“What the…” said Myra.

Liz quickly interrupted. “You better not say it, Myra. Yes, Sydney is bringing her kids this week. Clarence is not taking the kids, so I told her to bring them. And I also told her you will be okay and that you will get over it. Now, you see, Myra, there is something this week for everyone.”

“Girl! Please, Liz, get off this phone. I am about to hang up on you. Kids! Kids this week? I had already told you I was glad to be getting away from my sister’s kids, and now you tell me that Sydney’s kids will be there?”

“Bye.” Myra angrily hung up the phone.

Liz shakes her head in amusement. I guess Myra's little plan backfired on her, Liz thought.

Chapter Four
Stormy Weather

The ladies were all waiting at the airport for Daniel to arrive.
"Liz, did you call Sydney? Is Daniel here yet?"
"No, let me check." Rebecca's, phone rang. She looked desperately at Liz and stopped, "it is Matthew."
"Who is it?" whispered Liz.
"Matthew," whispered Rebecca.
"Ooh, give that phone to me, girl." Liz snatched the phone out of Rebecca's hand. "Go get the luggage and go to the car!"

"Hey, Matthew."
"Aha, Liz is that you?"
"Yes, Matthew, it is me, hey, right now Rebecca. Is getting the luggage and we are getting ready to meet Daniel."
"Okay. Wow, how are you, Liz? It is good to hear your voice. I know you ladies are so excited to see each other. Tell Becky I just called to make sure she got in safe and she can call me later when she gets a chance. I know you ladies will be talking all day. Hey, it's great talking to you, Liz."
"It was great talking to you too, Matthew. I will tell Rebecca what you said."
"Okay, bye, Liz." Liz turned with a smile, "Girl, it's all under control."
"Thanks so much, Liz. I know if I would have answered Matthew, he would have asked me questions and details. I didn't want him to know that Samantha is here yet."

"I understand, Rebecca."
"Hey, ladies."
"Liz, Rebecca and Samantha simultaneously quickly turned around with amazement, Daniel, Daniel, is that you?"
"Yes, ladies, it's me. I know. Do not say it! I am all grown up."
"Yes, yes, Daniel, you took the words right out of my mouth, it is really good to see you," said Rebecca.
"It's good to see all you lovely ladies too."
"Thanks for picking us all up," said Liz.
"Hey, ladies, just head right to the truck and I will get your luggage. Wow! Look at all this luggage! It is a good thing I am strong and I brought my truck. Are you guys going to the beach house or the South of France for a month?"
"Well, Daniel, if you think this is a lot, just wait until Myra arrives. You will need all of your strength and much more room," laughed Rebecca. "I think it would be best if you pick Myra up by herself because there will not be room for anyone else's luggage."
"Oh, yeah, look who is talking," Samantha whispered to Liz.
"Okay, Samantha, you know she is right," laughed Liz.
"No, Liz, just look at all the stuff Rebecca's got."
"Okay, Samantha, give it a rest. You know perfectly well we have the same number of bags."
"Yeah, Liz, but ours are not Louis Vuitton bags, just saying."
"Well, Samantha, I want you to stop just saying," said Liz.
Liz scooted into the truck and leaned forward to talk to Samantha in the front seat. "Samantha," whispered Liz, "you've got to get it together. It was ten years ago. Your

pettiness is a true sign of one or two things or maybe both. Is it your immaturity or you have not moved on or both?"
Samantha, quickly turned and looked out the window.
Rebecca entered the truck smiling and with excitement in her voice. "Okay, ladies, our fun journey starts now."
"Yes, yes, it starts, it starts. Isn't that right, Samantha?"
Samantha turned back and looked at Liz as she started jumping and smiling sarcastically. "Oh, yes, yes, girlfriends. We have started our fun journey," rolling her eyes at Liz as she turned around.
"Okay, ladies, I am your driver and I am to bring you to the house for Taylor's birthday party," laughed Daniel.
"Great!" shouted Liz. I really am excited to see Sydney's kids."
Daniel turned to the ladies and said, "Okay, ladies, make yourselves comfortable, sit back and enjoy the view because we have about a 50-minute drive depending on the traffic on the 405."

Myra called Belinda on the phone, "Hello, Belinda. Belinda, I am so glad I caught you." Myra sounded desperate. "Belinda, I got your number from Liz. We are on the same flight when I connect in Houston. I wanted to know if you would save me a seat with you on the plane?"
"Myra, Myra, the answer is no."
"What! Come on. I really need you to do this. Belinda, by the time I get off the plane and go to the gate you know all the good seats will be taken. Then I will end up sitting in the middle seat next to some big stinky man, which will be all your fault. So that's why I am asking you to save me a seat."

"Myra, Myra, do you ever listen to yourself? Now it is my fault if you get a middle seat on the plane. You are delusional, just delusional. Myra, goodbye, and I will see you in California."
"Ugh, bye, Belinda." Myra, quickly hung up the phone and whispered, "Belinda, gets on my last nerve."

Teddy is at home with his wife Sharon as they prepare to go to the airport. "Babe, Sharon, listen I am going to really miss you. Do you have to go? Why do you ladies have to go to this silly college reunion? All of you guys have been out of college for how many years? And most of you guys are wives and moms. Well, accept Myra. And no one in their right mind would marry her."
Sharon looks at Teddy, "Now, that's not nice to say, Teddy."
"Okay, Sharon, but honey, listen, it's a whole week and we are still newlyweds."
"Teddy, we have been married for six years we are not newlyweds."
"Teddy, baby, I will miss you too, but you will see, the week will go by fast."
"Not fast enough. Honey, I already miss you."
"Me too. Now, honey, you promised you will not let the boys stay up too late or eat tons of junk food. Promise me, Teddy."
"Give me another kiss, Sharon, and I will promise."
"Okay, Teddy, you are out of control. Here is your kiss. Now promise."
"Okay, I will promise after two kisses and a trip back to bed."
"Okay now you are trying to get me to miss my flight. Plus remember, we have to pick up Robert and Amanda."

"Sharon, let Robert take his own wife, and that will give us an hour. Then we can get back into bed."

"Teddy, come on, we are not telling Robert that. Did you forget we have to also drop the boys off at your mom's?"

"Ah, that's right. Okay, but we are really going to miss you, babe."

"And I will miss all my men too. Honey, let us get ready to go now. Teddy, get the boys into the car, and I am going to call Amanda and let her know we are leaving out."

"Hey, Amanda, we are leaving out now. We should get to you within the hour. But I will call you once we leave mom's house from dropping off the boys."

"Okay, thanks, Sharon. So you are on your way?"

"Huh, uh, no, Amanda, not for an hour or so."

Amanda turned and yelled to Robert, "Honey, Robert, they are on their way!"

"Huh, Amanda?"

"Okay, girl, I can finally talk. Robert talking about we are still newlyweds and stuff."

"Oh, okay, I understand, girl," laughed Sharon. "Teddy is singing the same song over here. They must have talked. Well, they are truly brothers. We just went through that at my house. We are on our way."

"Okay, bye."

"Hey, before you hang up have you heard from Liz?" Sharon interjects.

"Oh, yes, I have. Liz said we need to pray. She said stormy weather is ahead."

"Sharon, what could have possibly happened in less than 24 hours?"

Sharon recaps to Amanda, "well, girl, let me see, where do I start? First, Liz said Samantha, surprise everyone, who have sworn herself to be the arch enemy of Rebecca. Samantha unexpectedly showed up on the same flight with Liz and Rebecca. Next, Myra called and said she had it out with Belinda over plane seats. To top it all off, Sydney, the lady who owns the beach house, is upset and will probably not be joining us because her ex-husband changed his mind and will not pick up his kids for the week.

"What in the world is going on? And who is Myra and Samantha?" Asked Amanda.

"Girl, we will talk about it on the plane. It is too long of a story to go into now. Let us pray right now, because I can smell the rain and feel the drops. Stormy weather is not coming, it is here."

Belinda took her seat on the airplane when she heard her name being loudly called out. "Belinda! Belinda! screamed Myra, Hey save me a seat, save me a seat!"

Belinda looked up as she peeked over her seat and released a big sigh. "My goodness, why in the world is Myra frantically waving her hands at me and shouting out my name? God, please help me. Okay, okay, I hear you, Myra." Belinda shook her head and whispered. "It is going to be a long trip." Belinda's phone rang. "Hello, Liz, yes, I am on the plane. Uh, yes, Myra got here on time, and she screamed my name in front of all of these people like a mad woman asking me to save her a seat."

Liz responded. "Girl, no. Now, you might as well prepare yourself. Go get your fruit basket a.k.a. fruit of the Spirit, and get one of your favorites fruits and right now start eating. Make sure you have plenty to eat upon. Because Belinda, it is going to be a long trip," laughed Liz.

Belinda laughed too. "Yes, my goodness, you are so right. I just said that to myself just before you called."

"Hey, I called to check to see what time everybody will arrive so I can tell Sydney's brother, Daniel what time to be there to pick up everyone." Have you seen Sharon and Amanda?" asked Liz.

Belinda looked down the aisle. "No, Liz, not yet. Are they scheduled on this flight too?"

"I thought they were. Maybe I am wrong. Well, I need to find out so I can let Daniel know."

"Hey, wait, Liz, I see them. They are boarding right now. Okay, Liz, you are not going to believe this. I can hear Myra getting into it with Sharon." Belinda with the phone in her hand got up and quickly walked down the aisle as Myra approached her.

"Hold on, Liz. Myra, girl, wait. Myra, Myra, settle yourself down. I got your seat. What in the world is wrong with you?" Asked Belinda.

"Girl, no! I heard Sharon say, 'Oh, there is Belinda, we can sit next to her.' I just kindly, and I repeat, Belinda, I kindly said no. Belinda is saving that seat for me. But no, Sharon started looking at me like she did not understand what I was talking about. So I said it again just a little bit louder in case she did not hear me the first time."

"Myra, she heard you the first time, I know because I could hear you from where I was seated back there. Settle down. I told you I have a seat for you."

"Belinda, you know how-well, I just do not like sitting next to strangers on planes, blowing their bad breath and all close to me with their funky armpits and all."

"Wait a minute, Myra." Belinda returned to her call with Liz.

"Liz, Liz, are you still on?"

"Yes, Belinda. Okay, tell Myra to settle down or get her loud talking behind off the plane."

"Yes, put Myra on the phone," said Liz.

"Hey, Liz, I am on my way to you, girl. I got here just in time. We are supposed to be girlfriends forever, but Belinda didn't even try to help a girl out."

"Myra, uh, Myra," Liz tried to get a word in.

"Listen, Myra, bring it down, I mean all the way down."

"Girl, it's not me this time. It is your so-call cousins."

"No, Myra, it's you right now being so loud on that plane. Now, listen. We all have worked so hard for this week. We do not need any more drama or craziness. I am serious, or otherwise you can march your little behind right off the plane."

"Okay, yeah, yeah, Liz, I am all right. You know how I am about flying, sit-in' all close to these funky strangers."

"Myra, Myra, listen to yourself, ridiculous. Perhaps, just perhaps, the same people do not want to sit next to a loudmouth lady either. Have you ever thought about that?"

"Uh, what! Girl, no. I do not have a clue what you are talking about either."

"Myra, Myra, you do not have a clue. Listen, girl, I love you, but you got to stop being so loud and cantankerous."

"Loud and what? Can't, ah, what? Liz, I am not loud and whatever you said."

"Myra, Myra, come on, come on, we are grown women. Let us be real. It is time for a change, Myra."

"Liz, I hear you. I got to get off the phone. The plane is ready to go."

"Okay, we will talk later." With a glazed over stare, Myra slowly gave the phone to Belinda. "Liz, Liz, are you still there, whispered Belinda."

"Yes, I am."

"Hey, thanks, girl. See you in a couple of hours."

"Okay, I will pray for a safe flight for all."

"Thanks, bye."

Sydney, called Liz as she was riding in the car with Daniel.

"Hello, Liz, Liz, okay are you with Daniel?"

"Yes, Sydney, I am in the car, and we are on our way. I am so excited to see you and the kids. It has been a long time…,"

Sydney quickly interrupted Liz. "Wait, huh, hold on, Liz my house line is ringing."

Sydney picked up her other phone. "No, no!" screamed Sydney. "Clarence, you are not invited and no, no, and no, you cannot get them today! How dare you try to spoil Taylor's birthday party," screamed Sydney. "You are his dad!" screamed Sydney again. "Listen, Clarence, I am hanging up this phone. Do not call me anymore, do not come by my house or I will call the police. Just leave us alone."

Clarence yelled back, "Hey, Sydney, you cannot stop me from seeing my kids. I am coming and I have a right to get them."

Sydney screamed, "Clarence, if you come to my house, you will have the right to go to jail right in front of your kids. I am calling the police, so do not show up here. Stop calling me! We do not want to ever talk to or see you again."

"Sydney, listen, you are just tripping because I am not getting them this week. I am not a fool. You will have to see your man on your own time."

"What! Clarence, do you hear yourself? When you have the kids it is my own time, and I can do or see whoever I want."

"So yes, you finally admitted it," said Clarence.

"I-never mind. If you come to my house, you better be prepared to go to jail."

"Well, you better have the police ready, because I am coming to pick up my kids." Sydney immediately hung up the phone on Clarence.

"Liz, Liz, I am sorry. Are you there? Can you believe Clarence is wanting to come to Taylor's birthday party? If he shows up at my house, I am calling the police."

"Sydney, why is Clarence pushing this so far?"

"Hey, Liz, what is happening to Sydney? Is she and the kids okay?" asked Daniel. "What is that fool trying to do?" Let me speak to Sydney, now, Liz."

Liz handed the phone to Daniel. "Sydney, what is going on?"

"Hey, calm down, Sis, I got this. Hey, do not worry about him, Sydney. Just go back to planning Taylor's party. I will be there in a few. I will take care of it. No need to call the police. Remember what happened the last time, the kids were upset for months. I got it, Sis. Just finish with Taylor's party."

"Okay, Daniel, I will see you in a few."

"Yes, I will tell Liz that you are okay, bye." Daniel handed the phone back to Liz.

"Is she okay," asked Liz.

Daniel quickly dialed his phone. "Hey, man, I need you to take care of something for me. Can you get to my sister's house in 20 minutes? Cool. I will be there in about 30 minutes. Okay, bye."

Liz touched Daniel on the shoulder. "Is Sydney okay?"

"I am sorry, Liz. Yes, she is okay. I called a couple of my guys, and they are headed there now. All is good."

Rebecca gazed out the window and turned and whispered to Liz, "I want to help Sydney."

"What do you want to do, Rebecca?" whispered Liz.

Rebecca raise her head up from resting on the back of her seat and whispered to Liz, "I will tell you later, but I believe I can help Sydney and the kids."

"Oh, okay, Rebecca, tell me later."

Samantha whipped her head around and screamed, "Tell her what later, Rebecca? You and Liz have been whispering about me ever since we got on the plane, and I have had it. What in the world do you have to wait to say that you cannot say? Let us get this out in the open now! Tell me, Rebecca. Say it!"

"All right, Daniel," Liz said quickly. "Pull this car over right now. We are not going to bring all this ridiculousness to Sydney, who is already upset. Sydney is going through enough, and we are not going to bring her any more craziness. Pull the car over right now, thank you, Daniel! Get out, ladies, get out, and let us get something in order before we go one more mile."

Walking away from Daniel, Liz spoke in a firm voice addressing Samantha. Listen, Samantha, what in the world is your problem. Turning around and yelling at us and asking us what we were talking about? Then assuming we are talking about you, talking about you, Samantha. Listen to me when I tell you this, it is not about you, Sam. It's not about you."

"Well, why else would you and Rebecca be whispering? Liz, you know the situation between Rebecca, and me. So why would you and her whisper?"

"Okay, here's where you are wrong. There is not a current situation between you and Rebecca. And that is the problem, Sam. You knew perfectly well when you came on this trip that Rebecca would be here, so why did you come? Why did you come if you have not moved on or accepted the truth about a ten-year-old matter? No. Right now our only problem is you not acting like you are ten years older. Sam, you answer me. Why did you come? Because right about now you are not going to mess up my vacation. I have worked too long and hard for this week, and I do not think you really understand."

"Liz, first of all, you did not answer my question. Why did you and Rebecca feel the need to whisper?"

"Sam," Rebecca softly replied, "If you must know…

Sam rudely interrupted, shaking her head. "Yes, I must know."

"No," interrupted Liz. "Sam, she does not have to tell you what we were talking about."

"It's okay, Liz, I do not mind now that Daniel is not here. We were discussing how to help Sydney with the kids this weekend. I know she felt really bad about having to tell her kids they are not going with their dad. That is when you heard me say I will tell you later." Our conversation was not about you, and I am sorry you misunderstood us, Samantha."

At that moment silence filled the air and there was only the sound of cars rushing past the backdrop the playing for a few minutes.

"Samantha," quietly asked Liz. "Now, answer my question why did you come this weekend?"

Samantha slowly cast her eyes away from them and turned her back as she started to walk back to the car. She stopped and looked at the both of them with her eyes glazed over, put on her smoky dark shades and with a crackly voice she took a deep breath and whispered. "Liz, we said we were girlfriend's forever, and forever means here and now too."

As she walked away, Liz and Rebecca turned and stared at each other. Neither one uttered a word as they understood her. Liz turned and looked into the sky and prayed. "Lord, help us this week," as she started slowly walking to the car.

Rebecca agreed with a whispered, "in Jesus name, amen."

"Ladies, are you, all right? Are you ready now?" asked Daniel apprehensively as he looked at them.

"Yes, yes, we are all good," Samantha quickly answered. "We are going to the birthday party, and we will all have a great time. So yes, it is all good. We are all good; ladies do you agree?" asked Samantha.

Liz and Rebecca looked surprisingly at each other and smiled.
"Yes, yes," said Liz, 'I agree."
"I agree too," said Rebecca.
Liz turned and smiled at Rebecca and mouthed the words, "Thank you, Lord, for answering our prayers so fast."
"All right, ladies, how about some music? We got about thirty-five minutes before we get to the party, so once again, sit back, relax, and enjoy the scenery. Tell you what, ladies. I got the perfect solution to get you all beach ready. I will get off on the 405 and get on Route 1.
I know when you guys see the beach, it will put you back in vacation mood," said Daniel.
"How far does Sydney live from the Mission Impossible?" asked Samantha?"
"Uh, huh, Mission Impossible…Are you talking about my granddaddy's beach house?" asked Daniel.
"Oh, yeah, that's right, Daniel," laughed Liz. You never knew our nick name for your granddad's beach house. Altogether ladies, what's the word?"
"We are on a mission to have fun, and it will be impossible for anyone to stop us!" Suddenly the silence was broken and laughter quickly engulfed the truck.
"Hey, by the way, what is your name again?" asked Daniel.
"Samantha, but you can call me Sam."
"Okay, Sam. Well, Sydney, lives in Las Flores about thirty-five minutes depending on the traffic from uh, Mission Impossible," laughed Daniel.
"Daniel, do you live in Las Flores too?" asked Samantha.
"Uh, no, I cannot afford that. I live in Irvine."

"Okay, Daniel enough info," Liz sharply said.

"Whatever, Liz, I just know Sydney got it made. She got the bucks and lives with the rich folks."

"Okay, enough Daniel. I do not think Sydney would appreciate you discussing her business with us."

"Yeah, I am just saying, the girl got it made. Granddad left everything to her and her kids. I mean, a brother got a little, but he loved his great-grandchildren. My granddad always said that Sydney's ex, Clarence, is stupid. To think my granddad almost did not come to her wedding. But he told Sydney, Clarence, that fool, will never get a dime of his money. Well, he was right on all accounts.

"Again, Daniel, you are taking too much," said Liz.

"Uh, I heard you, Liz, I know. No wonder you and Sydney are friends. You guys are just alike. You never let a brother just flow."

Liz sighed and said, "Whatever, Daniel."

Liz quickly turned as she saw the ocean. "Oh, my goodness, now that is what I am talking about. Look at that water. It is so beautiful, I cannot wait, I cannot wait."

"I told you a brother knows how to brighten your day. Nothing better than Cali's beaches to make everything all right."

"Yes, yes, Daniel, you were so right. Thank you for the slight detour. It was so needed to refocus us back to why we are here. We are on vacation, ladies!" shouted Liz.

"Well, ladies, here we are. I hope you enjoyed your trip. I am expecting to be tipped the entire weekend. A brother does not come cheap, you know."

"Who are all these guys, Daniel?" ask Liz.

"Oh, sis, these are my boys. They are here to keep the peace."
"Daniel, your boys?"
Sydney, turned and screamed, "Oh, my goodness!"
"Yes, we are here!" screamed Liz from the truck. All the ladies leaped from the truck and ran, joined hands, formed a circle, and proceeded to jump, cry, and hug each other like children. Without notice, quickly Sydney's kids joined in the circle. Daniel looked on and laughed. "Wow, now, that is really special. Thank goodness for cameras on cell phones, this is priceless."
No one cared, no one heard him, they all just celebrated the moment. With tears in her eyes, Sydney spoke. "My girlfriends, I am so glad you are here. You are finally here."

Chapter Five
Mission Impossible

"Myra, Myra, wake up, we are here."

"What? Huh, what time is it, Belinda?"

"It's quarter to five."

Myra stretched as she prepared to get off the plane.

"My goodness, such a long trip, and I am so tired."

"Myra, you slept the entire trip," said Belinda.

"Yeah, but I have been packing and traveling all day."

Belinda shook her head as she reached for her overhead bag. Belinda smiled and said, "Myra, listen, we are here, and all I can think about is the beach and relaxation."

With disappointment in her voice Myra looked at Belinda, "Well, at least you can relax. Liz told me Sydney is bringing her kids. So much for relaxing."

"Ah, get over it, Myra." chuckled Belinda. "I believe we will not even notice that the kids are there. Besides, I am glad. This way I will get a chance to see them and spend time with them it will help me not to miss my boys so much."

Myra, shaking her head in utter disgust, "Missing kids? You just left them. What is wrong with you? Do not you want a break? Aren't you tired of your kids? I mean, really Belinda."

Belinda looked at Myra and laughed. "Myra, there is no need for me to try to explain it to you. One day you will know."

Myra stopped in the aisle turned, and looked back at Belinda.

"Oh, here is where you are wrong. No kids for me! I already know. Remember, I get my sister's bratty monsters. Mrs. Belinda, again, I say no, no!" Myra shook her head as she walked off the plane.

As Belinda passed Sharon, she asked, "Belinda, what is wrong with Myra now? Why is she shaking her head?"

Belinda laughed, "Girl, nothing, pay her no mind. Ladies, we have arrived, and let us just focus on why we are here. Sharon and Amanda, this is your first official trip to Mission Impossible, so get ready for a week that you will never forget. Get ready for the sun, lots of fun, great food, long days of relaxation, beautiful ocean, blue water, and just the task of doing nothing and I mean nothing. And ladies, you will not believe this! Sydney hired a chef, a housekeeper, a masseuse, and Daniel, Sydney's brother, is our chauffeur for the week. Well, ladies, get ready to be pampered and just enjoy being together."

"Oh, my, it sounds so wonderful I cannot wait," says Sharon.

"Yes, so dreamy, so dreamy." said Amanda.

Myra trailed behind the ladies as they walked to the baggage claim and whispered, "Well, if anyone asked me, it is a dream that will turn into a nightmare when the kids arrive."

"Hello, honey, how are you? I miss you already, Matthew."

"Hey, sweetheart, I miss you too. Are you at the beach house?"

"No, we are leaving now," said Rebecca.

"How was the birthday party?"

"It was great. You are so sweet, honey. He loved the signed jersey you gave him. Hey, honey I need your help."

"What is wrong, Rebecca?"
"Well, Sydney uh, wait, hold on Matthew."
"Okay, Sydney, I am coming. I will be there in a minute," yelled Rebecca.
"Clarence was supposed to take the kids this week so Sydney could go to the beach house. But some crazy disagreement has happened and now he will not take them this week as promised. Now Sydney is so upset and probably decided not to come because she does not want to bring the kids. She thinks it will ruin everyone's time here."
"Okay, Rebecca. What do you want me to do?"
"Well, I talked to Liz, who called Sydney's parents, who would love to have the kids for the week. I would love to surprise Sydney and fly them tonight to her parents. I know she would love that and feel better about coming."
"Great plan, Rebecca. No need to say more. Tell me when you want them to leave and I will arrange everything."
"Thanks so much, babe. I know it will mean the world Sydney. She has had the hardest day. I love you, Matthew."
"Love and miss you too. Hey babe, did all the ladies arrive?"
"Wait, hold on honey. Matthew, I am sorry, I got to go. Uh, I will text you the details."
"Okay, love you too, Matthew."
"Bye, love you, Rebecca."

Sydney called Daniel. "Daniel, tell the ladies that the car is here, so please bring the kids down to the car."

"Sydney, I tell you what. You ladies go on, and I will clean up here and bring the kids when I finish. This will give you all time to get settled in and stuff."
"Thank you so much, Daniel. I am so exhausted. If you could bring them in a couple of hours, that would be so great."
"No problem, Sis."

Sydney, called for her kids. "Hey guys, come and give mommy a kiss. I want you to help Uncle Daniel clean up, and mommy will see you after that. Love you."
"Thanks, Daniel, I truly love you for this. I really appreciate you so much for helping me out. Thanks for asking Tim and the guys to be here in case Clarence showed up. Love you."
"Love you too, now get going." Daniel smiled at Sydney.
As Liz and the ladies left, Daniel sent a text to Liz. "It's a go, so send me the details as soon as possible."

Liz's phone rang as she got ready to go to the car, and Sydney grabbed it.
"Okay, Liz, I got your phone." Sydney yelled. "Everyone listens up! No texting, we agreed. I know Robert can manage the office without you for one week!"
Liz reached desperately to get her phone back from Sydney. "Sydney, come on, give me back my phone. I am not working."
"No, Liz, I know you. I will keep the phone until we get to Mission Impossible. No work, remember, we all agreed."
Liz said with a frantic look on her face, "Okay, listen, Sydney, it's not work, so please give it to me and let me send one little text, and I will give it back to you."

Sydney shook her head and laughed. "No, no, Liz, I do not trust you. I will send the text. Okay, what is your text? Hey, what!"
Liz quickly snatched the phone back from Sydney. "I will do it. Here it goes. Sent. Phone locked, and you can have it." Liz gladly gave the phone back to Sydney.
Sydney yelled again. "Ladies, ladies, Liz cannot be trusted! Again, I repeat, ladies, Liz cannot be trusted! I will need everyone to make sure she does not work this week. Everyone is to watch her for me." Everyone laughed as they waited for the limousine to arrive.
Rebecca turned and winked at Liz. "Yes, yes," Rebecca said, "Sydney is right, everyone must watch Liz closely."

"Hey Daniel," texted Liz. "I just got a text from Rebecca, who said the pick-up time for the kids has been changed to five pm. Please have them at the airport by quarter past four. Here is Matthew's number if you need to contact him."
"Thanks, Liz," texted Daniel.
Daniel immediately called Matthew. "Hey, Matthew, my name is Daniel. I am such a great fan of yours, man, I mean a great fan. Matt, I really appreciate you doing this for my sister. Okay, thanks, thanks again man, good bye, Matthew." Daniel hung up the phone and whispered to himself, "I cannot believe it. I, Daniel, just talked to Matthew, the Matthew Whitfield, and I have his number."

"Listen up, everyone," yelled Sydney. "I really appreciate everyone being so kind and understanding about my kids being here this week. I really wanted to be here with you all, especially after seeing all of you. I will try to keep my kids out of everyone's way and hopefully they will not disturb you from having a great vacation."

"Sydney," said Liz, "Do not worry about it. We understand and we love you. It will be okay."

"I know, Liz, but I will talk to the others when they get here as well. I truly want to thank them too."

"Thank goodness the limousine is here. Myra, come on now," yelled, Liz. All the ladies grabbed their bags and hurried to the car. "Welcome ladies, welcome ladies, watch your heads. As the driver escorts each one of them into the car. "Welcome to California. We are headed to Newport Beach. There are cold beverages and refreshments inside, compliments of Mrs. Rebecca Whitman. Please help yourself, sit back, and we will be there in a few."

"Grandma! Grandma!" screamed Taylor and Trinity.

"Hey, Mom, they are all yours." said Daniel.

"Hi, son, thanks for bringing them."

"No, Mom, it's all good. Listen up you guys Uncle Daniel loves you, so give me a big hug before you go, and I will see you when you get back. Be good, you two."

"Grandma, where are all the people on the plane?" asked Taylor.

Grandma smiled as she picked up Taylor. "Oh, honey, this is what you call a private plane, and we are the only passengers besides the pilot and this lady, who will take good care of us on the plane. Come on and let us get seated. Your Grandpa is anxiously waiting to see you."

"Hey, Grandma, can we go fishing?" asked Taylor.

"Yes, Taylor, you can bug your Grandpa about fishing when you see him."
"Grandma, I love you."
"I love you too, Trinity."
"Grandma, mommy and daddy got into a fight and mommy did not want daddy to come to Taylor's birthday party. She was yelling and crying. Mommy said she would call the police if daddy came like last time."
"Trinity!" yelled Taylor, "Mom said we are not to talk about what is happening with her and daddy. Mom said you are just like Uncle Daniel with your big mouth."
Trinity cried out, "But it's Grandma Taylor, I can tell her."
Daniel turned and asked, "Hey, wait a minute, guys, what did she say about Uncle Daniel?"
Daniel's mom quickly interrupted him, "Daniel, be quiet."
"But Mom."
"Daniel! It is okay, Trinity, do not cry. It is okay, kids. Let us not talk about that right now. Right now let us enjoy this wonderful plane. Then we all can go see grandpa, and we will all have a great time. Okay, bye, Daniel."
"Uh, bye, mom. Love you and tell dad I said hi."
"Love you too, son, I will. When we land, I will call you."
As Daniel walked away, his phone rang. "Oh, my goodness, it's Sidney." Daniel said to himself, "No, no, my sister, you just have to wait."

Liz looked at Sydney on her phone. "Okay, Sydney, get off of your phone. Those kids are just fine with Daniel. Now who is working?"

"No, girl, this is not work, this is life. Besides, I am just checking on them."

"Sydney, the kids are all right. Look at this oh, my goodness, it's so beautiful."

Sydney stopped and gazed out the window. "Wow, Liz, it is so beautiful here. It is a real shame I live here, and I do not come out here more. When granddaddy was alive, I spent so many summers here with him. We had such great family times and memories here. Liz, I tell you, truly by the time I finish with the kids, I am overwhelmed and too tired to do anything. But it is time for a change. I need a new start, Liz, and this trip starts it off."

Liz clapped her hands in joy. "Yes, a new change is good Sydney, and it starts now."

Sydney's phone rang. "I am not going to answer this call. I wish Clarence would stop calling me." Sydney, turned to Liz and said, "Liz, I am going to answer his call for the last time today."

Sydney answered and yelled, "Clarence! What do you want? Why are you calling me? Uh, no, you cannot talk to the kids. Clarence, you need psychiatric care. This was supposed to be your week with the kids. But no, no, but because of your hatred towards me, you ruin the kid's opportunity to be with you. So no, no, again, no, you are not seeing the kids this week and do not call me again. Why do you keep telling me that they are your kids too when you do not act like their father? No, no, a real father would have picked them up and never broken his promise to them. A real father keeps his promise to his children. Clarence, did you ever think how they might feel when you decided not to get them because you were trying to stop me from supposedly seeing someone. Even though Daniel told you it was a lie, you still did not keep your promise to the kids. Listen, Clarence, even if it was the truth, me seeing anyone should not have stopped you from getting them. You are supposed to be their father. You are supposed to protect them from hurt. But no, you are their hurt. But I will not stand for you to keep on hurting them. Like you hurt me. Do not call me ever again, do not call the kids, and stay out of our lives. We are going through enough without you making things worse. "What?" Sydney stopped talking and took a deep breath. "One minute. I am listening, you have one minute, Clarence, and then I am hanging up. No, I am not listening to you saying you are sorry. Now you are sorry. No, I will not reconsider and I do not care how you feel. Now, is that all? What! Okay, you are certifiable-you are crazy, no!" yelled Sydney, and she hung up the phone. "Okay, I have heard it all. This crazy man said to me on this phone that he is still in love with me and that is why he did what he did. He is sorry and he wanted to get his kids. What a nut case. I am so mad. How could he ever think I would ever go back to him after all the things he has done to me and my kids? Talking about he just did that because he did not want me to see someone else. He thought about it and he does not want his kids calling another man dad. I cannot believe this is what he is worried about. He will not have to worry about that if he becomes the best dad in the world to them. I am getting so mad, the nerve of him to tell me he loves me. The man does not know the meaning of the words. I am so mad."

Samantha bumped Liz, "Girl, do something?"

Liz bumped Samantha, back, "Girl, just be quiet and let her have her say. Then she will be okay."

Sydney stopped and looked at Liz. "Sydney," Liz said softly, "Remember before that call, you were just talking about a new change starting now." Sydney stopped and looked around at everyone, took a deep breath. "Yes, I know, Liz, but you heard that nonsense from Clarence. Every time I try to move on, he does something so ridiculous and then wham! Here I am again. Now I am so upset. I need to get off this Ferris wheel with him. We keep going around and around, and I tell you nothing changes. Liz, I need things to change. I am sick and tired of being sick and tired."

Liz looked at Sydney. "Sydney, listen, we are about to go to your granddad's magnificent beach house that he gave for you and your kids to enjoy, and we will not let anyone stop us from enjoying this week."

Sydney sat and stared at the beautiful shoreline, then looked back at Liz and softly said, "Yes, yes. You, are right, Liz, it is time for a change. It is time for a change for me and my kids."

"Sydney, can we pray for you?" asked Rebecca.

"Sure, Rebecca. I need all the help I can get."

All the ladies bowed their head as Rebecca prayed. "Father, in the name of Jesus, we come to you first to tell you that we love you and with a heart of thanksgiving we bless your holy name. We stand in agreement, Lord, that you will bless Sydney and her family. I pray that salvation comes to this family. We agree that the Lord will bless Sydney and her family this week. We pray for new beginnings in you, Lord, for her life and her family. We pray for, the peace of God, to surround Sydney and her family. We pray that the Holy Spirit brings her into the knowledge of Jesus' love and the plans he has for her and her family. In Jesus name we pray, Amen."

Sydney lifted her head and smiled. "Thank you, guys, for praying for me. I feel better. We will have a good time. A new change is in store this week for me. Thank you, again, Rebecca, I feel better now."

"Yes, we will have a good time. The presence of the Lord is here now," whispered Rebecca.

"Yes, He is here with us." echoed Liz.

"Hey, hey guys, who is here?" asked Samantha.

"The Lord, that's who." Liz smiled as she answered.

"Oh, okay." Samantha suspiciously looked around. As they coasted down the beautiful 1 highway, silence filled the car as they enjoyed the view of God's creation and the peace of His presence.

"What in the world? Who is doing all that screaming? Liz, look it's Belinda and the others pulling up." said Belinda.

"Yep, Myra is loud as usual." Sydney turned and hugged Liz. "Thank you, Liz."

"For what, Sydney?"

"For convincing me to come. I really needed to be here. I have been so down about everything, and I have forgotten how to relax."

Liz turned to all the ladies, "Well, get ready, the best is yet to come."
"Hey, everyone, yes, yes, it's been too long. I have truly missed you all. Welcome to Mission Impossible!" shouted Sydney. "All together, ladies, what is the word ladies?" All the ladies chimed in and said, "We are on a mission to have fun and it will be impossible for anyone to stop us."
"Yes, yes, ladies," said Sydney. "Everyone come on in and let us get this vacation started."

Once again, Mission Impossible is filled with laughter, hugs, tears, and joy. The ten years that separated was the glue of their conversations. One by one, the ladies settled in. Liz quietly walked down to the golden beach shore, feeling the must needed warm sand in her toes. She smiled as she looked out upon the horizon, seeing the sun dawn quietly meeting the crystal blue ocean waves becoming as one. Liz finding a perching spot, sat down, and prayed and worshipped. Feeling a soft hand upon her shoulder, Liz turned and saw all the ladies quietly standing behind her staring at the wonder of God's creation.
"It is so beautiful," whispered Myra, "so beautiful."
Liz turned with tears in her eyes. "Thank God, I have found the answer, and it is the ocean."
"What are you talking about?" asked Sydney.
"Did you hear Myra?" She whispered."
Everyone turned and looked at Myra, then silence quickly erupted into laughter.
"Yes, that is it Myra. You are moving here."

"Ah, be quiet, you guys are a mess. Come on, I am hungry, let us go to the house because something smells so good. I want to see what that good-looking Chef Rio has cooked up for us."
Liz turned to Myra and said. "Okay, there you, go, Myra. Do not go in there hitting on the Chef. He is here to do a job, so do not ruin it."
Myra turned and asked Sydney. "Hey, Sydney, is the chef a man with a job, right?"
"Is that all your requirements that you, have for a man, Myra?"
"Okay, let me ask you, Mrs. Belinda. Do not you have a man, and does he have a job?"
"No, I do not just have a man with a job. I have a man of God with a job. There is a big difference, Ms. Myra."
"Whatever. I am not trying to put God in this, Belinda."
"Why not," screamed Liz and Rebecca.
"Okay, I see right now it's time to team up on Myra. Forget it, I am going inside to eat."
Sydney laughed and said, "Well, let us go ladies so we can save the Chef."
Liz laughed too. "Yes, yes, let us go and save the Chef."

Sydney's phone rang. "This must be Daniel with the kids. No! I am not answering it. It's Clarence again."
Liz, Rebecca, both yelled, "Do not answer it! Put your phone away, Sydney."
"Hey, I will, let me first call Daniel to see where he is with my kids."
"Okay, Sydney, you can call him after dinner. This gives you a chance to do something you have not done in a long time.

That is to have dinner without your kids. Remember we just said new changes."

"Liz, you are right, let us eat. I will call him after dinner."

Liz turned to Belinda. "Please pray for the food, girl."

"Sure, Liz. Lord, we thank you for this incredible feast that is set before us. We thank you for the blessing of friendship. We asked that you bless our food and our stay in Jesus name. Amen."

Myra turned to Belinda. "Girl, Belinda, you prayed so long the food is getting cold. Why did you need to pray so long? Do not you know a sister needs to eat?"

Liz laughed and turned to Myra. "Do we need to drag you back to the ocean again, to get you to be quiet?"

"Ha, ha, ha, funny Liz," Myra sarcastically said. "Just pass me the mushroom risotto. It looks so good."

"Everything looks and smells so good. Thank you, Chef Rio!" shouted Samantha."

"Listen, ladies, since we are all here, I need to speak to you. I know all of you know about my situation with my kids."

"No," as Liz, interrupted Sydney, "it is not necessary."

Sydney, quickly interrupted Liz. "I know, Liz, but let me finish. I want to first thank Liz for talking me in to coming. I truly have missed all of you, and I am looked forward to spending the rest of the week with everyone. As you know my brother, Daniel, will bring my kids soon. I want to thank all of you for being so kind and understanding about my kids being here this week. I will try very hard to keep them out of everyone's way. I feel a little bad about them being here, and I want to especially thank you, Myra, for your understanding too."

Myra looked around at all the ladies, holding up her palms. "Me, why me? I am all right."

"What!" shouted Liz. "Myra, you have made it perfectly clear to everyone here how you feel about kids."

"Uh, well, it is okay, I guess. Again, why is everyone teaming up on me?"

"Okay, Myra. I am just playing with you," laughed Liz.

Sydney's phone rang again. "I am sorry, just ignore that. When Daniel gets here with my kids, I will turn it off. I am not sure what is wrong with Clarence and why he keeps calling. But as soon as my kids get here, I promise off goes my phone."

Liz turned to Sydney. "Well, Sydney, we have something to tell you. Sydney, we appreciate your concern for all of us. But our concern is for you. I know if the kids come this week, they would not have much fun bumming around with us old folks."

"Wait a minute, who is old?" shouted Myra. "Speak for yourself, Liz."

Liz laughed and pointed to the view of the ocean from the deck. "Myra, stop interrupting."

Liz turned to Sydney, and continued. "Well, ladies, we are all old compared to her babies."

Myra turned away from Liz and whispered. "I am not old no matter what."

Liz shook her head at Myra. Liz turned once again to Sydney. "Okay, your kids will not be joining us this week."

Sydney jumped up and shouted to Liz, "What are you talking about, Liz? What is going on? Where in the world are my kids?

You better not tell me, Elizabeth Irene Marshall, that you gave my kids to Clarence or I will..."

Liz said with her hands stretched out to Sydney, "Hold on, Sydney. Now you know I would never do that. Now, sit down and Rebecca. I will tell you the rest."

Rebecca smiled and looked at Sydney. "Girl, I too love your kids, but having kids myself I know they would be bored crazy hanging out with us. So Liz and I contacted your parents, and they are with them."

Sydney looked around at everyone in total unbelief and slowly sat down. "What? How? When? Are you kidding me? How did you do this? My parents live in Kentucky. How did you get them there?" With tears in her eyes. Sydney turned and asked, "Rebecca, Liz, how did you all do this?"

Rebecca got up and sat next to Sydney. "We got Daniel to take them to the airport, and Matthew flew your mom in to meet them and flew them back to Kentucky."

In silence Sydney looked at her friends as tears streamed down her face, staring in utter unbelief. "I do not know what to say, uh, thank you, guys. Rebecca, I do not know how to thank you and Matthew." Sydney sighed and looked at all the ladies. "Everything has been so hard, and I have just been a mess. It has been a long time since anyone took care of anything for me, not since my divorce. I am so sorry. I do not mean to cry and mess up everyone's dinner."

Rebecca reached and hugged Sydney. "It is all right; we are all here for you."

"Yes, we all love you," cried Belinda.

"Okay, ladies, enough of the tears," joyfully said Myra.

"Look, we got great food, so let us eat and celebrate the kids having fun with the grandparents. Let us lift your glasses high, ladies, and let us give a cheer for the best news ever."

"Oh, now you want to celebrate, Myra," asked Belinda. "What a change of tone for you since on the plane earlier." Belinda chuckled and looked at Liz.

Liz turned to the ladies. "Okay, ladies, I appreciate Myra's sarcasm. Let us do exactly what she said. Raise your glasses high and let us toast to Mission Impossible, to girlfriends forever." Enjoying great food, the ladies told their stories of ten years that so quickly passed by. Liz sat back and looked around the room. Observing all of her friends, she thanked God for them, this place, and the moment she was enjoying right now in her life.

"Liz, Liz, wake up, wake up." said Myra. "Myra, what are you talking about? Why are you waking me up? Myra, listen, I was the only one willing to share a room with you. Do not make me regret it. What time is it?"

Myra walked over to Liz's bed and bent down and said, "You will not believe it. It is ten a.m."

"What! Ten a.m. Stop fooling," said Liz.

"Yeah, it's ten a.m., and you are missing the beach, Ms. Sleepy Head."

"Who else is up?" asked Liz.

Myra walked to the bedroom window. "I am not sure. From here I see Belinda, Sharon, and Rebecca, sitting together and reading their books."

"No, Myra, they are reading their Bibles." Liz put her pillow over her head.

"Hey, I do not see Amanda. She must be still sleeping in or at breakfast. But wait, there is someone. Ooh, girl, Liz, we are missing it! Get up, get up! There are two very, very, and I mean really fine men talking with them. We got to get out there!"

"Myra, settle down. What are you doing?" As Liz turned over in her bed.

"Girl, Liz, all them out there are a bunch of old married women. Liz, listen to me, we got to get down there right away so they will have a reason to stay around. I bet they are so selfish that they are not telling them that there are four very eligible fine ladies in the house. We got to get out there before they leave, Liz," shouted Myra. "Get up and get dressed!"

"Myra, you, go on and save all of us single ladies, but I am going to lay here a little bit longer and then get up and enjoy the good smelling breakfast Chef Rio made."

"Wait, oh, my goodness, no way, you will not believe it Samantha is heading out there now. Liz, are you listening? Myra put on her clothes and quickly brushed her hair as she looked at Liz.

"No, go on, Myra, please let me sleep." As the door quickly shut Liz peeked out of her beach front window and laughed as she saw Myra swiftly walking across the hot sandy beach leaving a dusty trail. Liz shook her head and laughed as she got back into her bed.

"Hello, my name is Myra, and you are?"

In utter amazement everyone turned around.

"Well, well, good morning, and yes, this is Myra." said Belinda.

"Hello, my name is Joseph Strauss, nice to meet you."

"I am Brad Bishop and good morning to you."

"Nice meeting you too. Are you guys from around here?" asked Myra.

"Yeah, we are. We are expecting a couple more guys who will be here in a few." said Joseph.

"Hey, that's great, one big party," said Myra.

"Hey, speaking of a party. At noon we are having a birthday party for one of our friends. If you can, please come by." asked Brad.

"Great!" shouted Myra. "A party the first day we are here. Sure, we would love to come."

"Uh, thanks so much, guys, I believe I can speak for everyone here." said Sydney, as she looked at Myra. "We have plans, Brad. Thank you for your invitation."

"Hey," Myra yelled out. Belinda side kicked Myra.

"Hey, thanks, guys." said Sydney.

"Okay, well, thanks for the Bible lesson. Hopefully, we will see you ladies at the birthday party, or if not, we will be here in the morning again." Brad and Joseph left.

"What is wrong with you, Myra?" asked Belinda.

"Me? Listen, you guys are a bunch of old married Bible thumping women. I do not have a husband or a man, so I need to take advantage of every, and I mean every, opportunity. So do not kick me, Mrs. Belinda, and get out of my way." Myra turned and walked away. “By the way, I am going to that party. Are you with me, Sam?”

“I am with you, girlfriend.” said Samantha as she walked away with Myra.

Belinda turned to the ladies. “Now, ladies, like I informed you before, if you fool with Myra, you will have to use all the fruit of the Spirit, then make a fruit salad, and then eat it all at once.”

All the ladies were laughing as Liz approached. “Hey, what's wrong with Myra? What is she talking about saying, “Let her kick me again and old married Bible toting women?”

Belinda quickly turned and looked at Liz, “Trust me, you do not want to know. It is good you were not here. But forget about that. Sit down with us. We are almost finished with our study in John Chapter 15.

“Lunch was so delicious; I am so full, Liz.”

“So am I, Sydney. I want to sit here on the beach the rest of the day.”

Amanda approached the ladies. “Hey, what is everyone doing?” asked Amanda.

“Are you just getting up?” asked Sydney.

“Yeah, for some reason I am so tired and sleepy. Did I miss the Bible study?”

“Yes, girl, that was hours ago. We are getting ready for our massages,” said Belinda.

“Yes, oh, I cannot wait,” said Amanda as she turned to Sharon. “I am really looked forward to that too.”

“Me too, Amanda. I really needed a vacation. I have not had a vacation since I got married. Teddy and I have been so busy with the boys and now building a new house. I think I am just on autopilot. Now I am feeling bad for enjoying myself so much. Now I am missing Teddy and my boys."

"Sharon, I am feeling the same way," said Belinda. "My day is also just filled with soccer, football practices, homework, children's ministry, and how can we forget Mark's honey nights," laughed Belinda.

"Yes, ladies, I totally understand. The same here, kids, school, games, practices, children's ministry, and church stuff," said Rebecca."

"Yeah, but Rebecca, you got a lot more stuff to do because of Matthew. I see all those special appearances, travel, and media stuff. I pray for you always," said Belinda.

"Girl, thanks for your prayers, Belinda, I really need them. And like you all, after all is said and done, I still have to take care of all those honey nights." said Rebecca.

"I do not know how you guys do it. It is just Robert and I, and I am whipped by the end of the day." said Amanda.

"I cannot imagine you with kids either, being married to my brother, Robert. I even feel sorry for Sharon too. Both of my brothers are so demanding of your attention." said Belinda.

"Yeah, you are right, Belinda," said Sharon.

Belinda shook her head. "I am surprised my brothers parted with you guys for a week."

"Yes, let me look and see if they are hiding in the water or something," laughed Liz. "Amanda, you got your hands full with Robert. I do not know what will happen if you have a baby. I asked Robert just last week, 'When are you going to have a baby?' He said he was not ready yet. Listen, the big baby said I want to enjoy my wife first. I do not want to share her with anyone right now."

"Is that what he said?" asked Amanda.

Amanda smiled at the ladies, "Well, Robert got me all by himself for the next seven months."

"What!" screamed Sharon.

"What!" screamed Liz. "Are you telling me I got a new baby cousin on the way!" shouted Liz.

"No, Liz, you have two new baby cousins on the way."

"What, twins!" screamed Rebecca. "Why didn't you tell us? How do you feel? No wonder you slept in." Rebecca danced in excitement.

"So I take it that Robert does not know yet?" asked Liz.

"No, he does not know," said Amanda.

"Belinda, did you know?" asked Liz.

"Yes, Liz, but she didn't tell me. I cornered her when I noticed how sleepy she has been."

"When are you going to tell Robert, Amanda?"

"I will tell him after this trip. My thinking is, by the time I get back he will be so glad to see me and miss me so much he will not care what I say to him," laughed Amanda.

"Yes, that will do it," laughed Sharon.

"Guess what, ladies, it is baby shower planning time." said Sharon.

Myra and Sam returned to the beach and found all the ladies in excitement.

"Hey, what is all the celebration about?" asked Myra.

"Well, you missed the announcement. Amanda is having twins. Isn't that great, Myra?" asked Liz.

“Oh, uh, okay, can we just have a week without kids either in or out of the womb? Ladies, let us get things straight. Did not we come here to have fun, to get away from kids and all that stuff? But since this morning all you guys have been doing is just sitting around talking about your kids, doing Bible studies, sleeping in, and not attending this great party next door. Why did you all come here?”

“Remember Myra,” said Belinda pointing at all the ladies, “We all came here to be with each other and not to get away from our kids, who we adore, nor our husbands, who we love. We came to spend time together as dear girlfriends. So you are right. We did not come here to party, but to spend time with each other. So if you and Sam want to go to the party next door, go right ahead and have a good time. But do not try to put us down because we are doing what we came here to do , to be with each other. So I guess the question we should ask you, is why did you come, since you do not have kids or a house to get away from?”

Myra turned around and walked toward Belinda, only to be stopped by Liz. “All right, Belinda,” said Myra. “You do not have to talk that way to me. Just because I do not have a husband or kids does not mean I am less than you guys.”

“Well, Myra I didn’t say that. But I believe right about now is a perfect time for you and Sam to go to your party.”

Myra took a deep breath, turned, and looked at Liz. “Okay, Liz, but remember, I am not the one.”

“Okay, Myra, we all know you are not the one. Listen, you, look awesome, so go on to the party. We will talk later.”

"Yeah, girl, I know I look good. Come on, let us go Sam. Let us leave them to whatever they are doing. We will see you later."
Myra stormed off with Sam across the sandy beach.

"Now, where were we? Yes, yes, Amanda, you are going to be a mom. I know you are so excited," said Rebecca.
"Yes, I am excited, but I am also a little nervous too, guys. Twins? Whatever am I going to do? And I am not sure about this being great news for Robert. One baby, but two? I am not sure, ladies. You will have to pray for us. I am not sure how he will take the news."
"Girl, it will be okay. You will have plenty of help. There is me, Liz, Sharon, Mom, and do not worry about Robert. He will be all right after he gets over the initial shock," laughed Belinda.
"Bahahaha," laughed Liz, "I bet he makes me a partner, and then he will have to hire another assistant. This is so God! Robert cannot be so selfish anymore, not with twins on the way."
"You are so right, Liz, this is just such a God thing, to pull Robert out of that me and mine attitude." said Belinda.
"Hey, stop beating up on my husband," laughed Amanda. "I declare he will get better, in Jesus name."
"Well, I tell you I stand in agreement with you Amanda, because he cannot help but to get better," laughed Belinda.
"Amanda," said Belinda, "since we are all together, it is a perfect time to plan the baby shower."
"Yeah, that sounds fun. Let us do it." said Amanda.

Meanwhile, Amanda's husband picked up the phone and called his friend, Matthew.

"Hey, Matt, how are you hanging?" said Robert.

"Hey, Robert? Okay, you know."

How are you doing?" asked Matt.

"Matt, I am missing my baby like crazy. We are only on day two, and I am not sure I can take this for another three days. I am about to jump up and go down there and bust up that girl gathering and take my wife and bring her home. I cannot sleep at night, Matt. This is too long, man."

"I know, my thoughts exactly. It is something, man. Most of my career I have traveled. But when I am on the off-season, I want her here home with me. I guess I really know how she feels when I am gone. I am going nuts. This really teaches me to appreciate her more."

"I know. I spend long hours at the firm while Amanda is at home too. I got to do better. You know, this is the first time we have been separated since we were married." said Robert.

"What! Robert, how long have you guys been married?" asked Matt.

"Six years." said Robert.

"It's been six years since the wedding? Wow, where has the time gone? And you guys have never been separated?" asked Matt again.

"No. I mean, during the day when she goes to see her mom, but that's it."

"Hey, when do you guys plan on having some little ones? Man, you are not getting any younger." laughed Matt.

"I do not know. Matt, I love kids, but if I am struggling to find time for Amanda, What will happen if I have kids? You know, man."

"No, man, I do not know. Robert, you know my wife talked to Liz. She said Amanda has asked you for years to add Liz as your partner. Since Liz just finished taking the Bar, are you going to bring her on as a partner?"

"Yeah, Matt, right now I got things running smoothly. I do not have time to bring in a new associate and get him or her familiarized with all the workings of the firm."

"Man, you know Liz will do that. Besides, I am telling you, your wife will not wait forever to have a baby."

"Wait, man, uh, are you trying to tell me something? Does Rebecca know something?" frantically Robert asked Matt.

"No, man, I am just saying, I thought the same way. I am gone at least six months out of the year, and I felt I did not have time for her, let alone kids. But Becky said she is not having babies in her forties."

"Matt, how do you do it with two kids? I mean, I love kids, but where do I find the time to properly raise them? My mom and dad were there for us. But times have changed, and I do not have that same luxury. I have to run my business."

"Robert, I am telling you that you need a new partner for your firm. Well, it would go well if you would check with your wife, she may have different plans on kids."

"I got to pray about this partner stuff, and I guess a baby too." said Robert.

Matt laughed, "Hey, man, you do not need to pray about no baby stuff. Now you know how to do that."

"I know man, but how do you do it? Things are so bad. How do you not worry about the safety of your kids?"

"Robert, you know I trust God, but I keep my peace makers with me for those who do not want to trust God," laughed Matt. "But on the real. I pray all the time for my family. Especially, because of what I do. I ask God and the angels to watch over my family."

"Remember when I was drafted?" asked Matt.

"Yeah, I remember," said Robert.

"When Becky and I married, uh, hey, I never told you this, but do you remember Samantha Reed?"

"Samantha who?"

"When we were in college, you know, the girl from Emerson Hall."

"Matt, I vaguely remember her."

"Well, after Becky and I married this girl stalked us."

"What! Why! When!" asked Robert.

"This girl stalked us for three years. She would show up at my games, even out of town games. She also called Becky over and over I changed her number countless of times. I do not know how she got her number. She even called crying to my parents."

"Man, what did you do to that girl?" asked Robert.

"Here's the thing, man, I never had a romantic relationship with her."

"Yes, I remember in college I remember you were doing the Jesus thing way before any of us were doing it. I did not tell you then, but you were my inspiration. I mean, in college we were out there; you would try to talk to us about the Lord and the Bible, but we were too far gone. It was college, and we were so dumb back then. But all of us knew that you were the real deal. I still remember the day you signed, live on TV. We all jumped and screamed, yes! We were all so excited for you. We were also relieved once you told us you were going to marry Becky. She was the perfect lady for you. So man, what is the deal with this Samantha? And why didn't you come to me for legal help? I would have handled it for you."

"I know, Robert, that you would have, but Becky did not want to bring the law into this. You see her and Samantha were friends. Matter of fact we were all friends. She was cool back then. We hung out together all the time. I thought we were good friends, but…"

Robert quickly interrupted, "But do not tell me she took your friendship as something more, right?" ask Robert.

"Yes." Matt dropping his head. "Robert, things turned crazy," said Matt.

Robert shook his head, "I do not know why women always do that. It is hard to be friends with them without them thinking more. If I do not hit on you, then we are just friends and nothing more. I do not know why they do not understand that," asked Robert.

"Well, like I said, when I first dated Becky, she wanted to keep our relationship a secret because she wanted to seek God about it. I understood. Man, after Becky gave me the green light. I expressed to her I wanted her as my wife and not just as a girlfriend. I let her know that I loved her and I wanted her to be my wife."

"Man, you were wise, because she would not be around long. She was one of those rare ladies like my Amanda, who knows who she is, who handles herself with nothing but class, and no two-bit brother will turn their heads. Yeah, you better had locked that up. Because you knew it was the end of college, and the brothers were circling. And she was in the circle."

"I know, man. I loved Becky from day one. But I did not want to scare her off. Since Samantha and I were high school buddies, I thought it was a perfect way for me to meet Becky. Wow, what a mistake. This girl went loco and came unglued once I told her I was going to ask Becky to marry me. She accused me of being deceitful and a snake and just using her. Man, she lost it."

"Yep, that's how those types are." said Robert.

"I thought the drama was over with, but after the wedding she took it to another level of madness." said Matt.

"Robert, I never imagined she would go so far. I had to hire a guard for my wife and family. Becky would come to games and bring my kids, and this deranged girl along with some of her crazy girlfriends would scream out things at Becky, throw things at her man, it was too much. At a final attempt, before we moved to getting the law involved, Becky asked me if the three of us could meet. I agreed."

"What happened?" asked Robert.

"You would never believe it. Becky called Samantha on the phone to ask her to meet with us to see if we could put closure to this matter before she took legal steps. Samantha said, no, it was unnecessary, we were not that important to her. We needed not to worry. She would never speak to either of us again, or she hung up the phone."

"Man, wow, just like that? Hey, did she keep her word? Have you guys heard from her again?"

"Gratefully, no, we haven't. However, one day at little Matt's birthday somebody called and cursed at Becky, but you know Becky she just hung up the phone. But other than that, it's been quiet and we have never talked or seen her again."

"Man, you are right. That was some crazy stuff." said Robert.

"Yeah, God had to give me peace. I said to the Lord. This is my wife, my life, please do not let anything happened to her. She is the love of my life. When I met Becky, I knew she was the one for me forever, man."

"I know, that's the same way I feel about Amanda." Robert stood up. "Listen, Matt, I am going to go and get my wife." eagerly said Robert.

Matt quickly interrupted Robert, "Hold up and settle down. I tell you what. Let us use tonight to pray about bringing on a new partner so you can free up time to go and make some babies."

laughed Matt.

"Yeah, you are right. I planned on bringing Liz on as a partner when she gets her results from the Bar. However, when I do that, I will have another problem. I will need to find another office assistance/paralegal, which in my mind is impossible. Liz is the greatest. Now, finding a replacement for Liz will be almost impossible. This is another reason why I am going nuts this week. "Matt, both of them are gone. Man, what in the world was I thinking? My life is a mess both here and at home.

"Robert, it will be all right," laughed Matt. "We got to be strong, we are men. Okay, man, Robert, who am I kidding. I feel the same way. But we cannot go there."
"I know," said Robert. "But I am really tempted, and I tell you, if I cannot go to sleep tonight, I might be singing a different tune in the morning," laughed Robert. "By the way, Matt, I called you to see if you checked your schedule. Are you going to be able to do a presentation at the church for the men's gathering at the end of the month?"
"Oh, yeah, man, it's cool. I can be there. Just email me the info and I will be there, and I got the media stuff too." said Matt.
"Thanks, Pastor Carlton will be so excited."
"No, I got it. It is all good. You know P.C. is my man. Tell P.C. I will see him the next time I come to Houston."
"Okay, man, now go to sleep, Robert. I will hit you back later."
"Yeah, Matt, man, you do the same, later."

Myra and Sam were next door at Brad's beach birthday party.
"Sam, I am telling you, when we get back, I am going to have a long talk with Ms. Belinda. She always put me down and she said she is a Christian. Well, Christian or not, I am going to give her a piece of my mind. Just because I am not married or do not have kids, it does not make her better than me," Myra said angrily.
Sam leaned close to Myra, "I think you do need to talk with her, but I would wait until she is alone. Otherwise, all of them may gang up on you."
"Let them jump in, Sam. I do not care. All of them heard Belinda downgrade me, and I am not going to tolerate it. She

always acts like she is holier than thou. Well, she is not. Look how she acted when I called her and asked her to save me a seat on the plane. She had an attitude. No, that was the last straw. Let us go on to this party, girl, but sister, gal, is going to be dealt with when we get back."
"Okay, Myra, I am with you, girlfriends forever."
"Ooh, girl, look at these cars here. Sam, we have hit the jackpot. Come on. We have found the treasure chest. Let us just play it cool when we get inside."

Myra and Sam excitedly entered the party
Hey, come on in, you are the ladies from next door. Uh, let me guess. You are Rebecca or Belinda?" asked Brad.
Myra frowned, "No, I am Myra, and this is Samantha."
"Oh, oh, I am so sorry. Yes, that is right. Welcome Myra and Samantha, and come in and meet everyone."
"Wow, Myra, he did not even remember our names," whispered Sam.
"Well, nothing is wrong with that. I did not remember his either."
"I did." smiled Sam.

Liz and Sydney relaxed on the beach. "I have forgotten how beautiful and peaceful the nights are here. Back in the day, we were so busy partying and running, we were totally ignorant of the tranquility of being here." said Liz.
"Yeah, Liz, I feel the same. Right now I want to lay here and wish all my problems away. I wish it were possible. I wish Clarence would just go away anywhere. I wish I could just get my life together. Liz, I have been a wreck ever since the

divorce. I have not found a new normal. I feel I just keep pressing on into the next responsibility. You know, it is so funny that Clarence did not keep his kids because he thought I was having a week get-a-way with a man. I thought, I am thirty-something, do not say anything, and I do not even have a boy that is a friend, let alone a boyfriend," laughed Sydney. "I tell you it is just pitiful, Liz, just pitiful."

"Okay, thanks, Sydney. I thought you were my friend, and now you are saying I am pitiful too."

"Huh, girl, what are you talking about?"

"I am thirty-something and do not have a boyfriend too. So, according to your definition, I am pitiful too because we have the same status."

Sydney looked at Liz and sighed deeply. "Liz, I know, but you're different."

"How am I so different, Sydney?"

"For starters, you do not have two kids and a crazy baby daddy."

"Sydney is that it?" asked Liz.

"No. Really Liz, you appeared to have peace about being single. I believe I would too if I did not have kids. Well, I do not know. Many days I am so busy, Liz, I have not had the time to even think about how I feel until now. All I know is I need something. I have not felt good inside since my divorce. Maybe this is how I should feel Liz. I do not know." Sydney laid back on her lounger and looked into the deep blue sky filled with twinkling stars and whispered, "Liz, I simply do not know."

"Liz, well, Sydney, I do have peace, but it has nothing to do with me being single. No, no, Sydney I have peace now because I want God more than anything. This was something I learned the hard way. About the same time you were going through your stuff with Clarence, I was walking through the peril of being rejected three days before my wedding to Tony." Sydney quickly turned to Liz.

"Oh, Liz, I am so sorry. I didn't mean to bring up bad feelings."

"No, no, Sydney, I am not feeling bad."

"You are not? Girl, why do you have that smile on your face?" asked Sydney.

Liz turned to Sydney, "Let us take a walk for a while."

"Sure, Liz, let us walk," said Sydney.

"Listen, Sydney, what happened to me that day turned out to be one of the greatest blessings in disguise. Back in the day, I thought I had a relationship with God. Until this crisis hit my life. When Tony called off the wedding, my life fell apart. I mean, it went into a tailspin and flung somewhere into outer space. I lost it. I could not think, eat, sleep, work or do anything. I blamed everyone, Tony, my friends, and even God. I decided that I would not speak to God and that we were done. My thinking was that God, you let me down. But you, see Sydney, in reality, I didn't even know God."

"What do you mean? You always went to church, so why are you saying you did not know God?"

"Yes, you are right, Sydney, I did always go to church, and I am ashamed to say. I knew nothing about God. When I tell you, Sydney, I knew nothing, I mean nothing. After what Tony did to me, I was determined to fix my own life. Which led me to doing more stupid things. Do you know in desperation I went to Eric to get advice on men?"

"Ooh, girl, yes, you were out there," laughed Sydney.
"It is the truth," laughed Liz. "My goodness, I was so out there, all the while being mad at God. I am so grateful God's love looked pass my foolishness, because I was so out of my mind. After Eric's advice left me looking silly on the train home, I decided I needed a new start. I decided I am the captain of my own ship. I told myself I needed new surroundings, a new job, and no more boring long train rides to and from work. I wanted to start over again. That was what I needed. So I went crazy and quit my job, and I stopped trying to get Tony to marry me, moved back to my hometown, moved in with my cousin Teddy, got a job with my cousin Robert, started back to school, and started my life over again. Now here is the amazing part. After doing all of that, guess what happened? I ran right back into God," laughed Liz.
"What do you mean you ran right back into God? I thought you already went to church and stuff."
"I did, but I did not know God."
"Wait a minute, Liz, going to church is knowing God, right?"
"Yes and no, Sydney. Yes, you can attend church and know God, but you can also attend church and not know God."
"But why would someone waste their time going to church if they do not believe there is a God?"
"You are off subject, my dear. I always believed there was a God, but just believing does not mean that you know who God is."
"You are confusing me now, Liz." Walking close to Sydney, Liz sat with her in the sand. "Sydney, listen, to believe in someone and to know someone is two different things. When I

found that out, that is when I got the great peace that I am telling you about. Sydney, do you believe that Amanda is married to my cousin, Robert?"

"I do," said Sydney curiously.

"Okay, now tell me, Sydney, what do you know about their marriage?"

"Well, uh, I, know nothing about their marriage. Come on, Liz, what does Amanda and Robert's relationship have to do with me knowing God?"

"You said you believed they were married, yet you knew nothing about their marriage. Sydney, to just believe is not an end in itself. We must go to the next step and know God."

"But Liz, who really knows God? I mean, He is God."

"I know God, and guess what, God wants us not only to believe but to know Him. Matter of fact, Sydney, God expects us to know Him."

"He does? But how to we get to know God?"

"The same way you would get to know about Amanda's marriage to Robert, by…"

"I get it," interrupted Sydney, "by spending time with her and talking with her."

"Yes, Sydney. When you spend time with her, you get to know her more and more."

Sydney signed deeply, "Oh, Liz, you are so right. I cannot tell you the last time I picked up my Bible or went to church or anything. The only time I come to God is when I am troubled, but you are right. I do not even know if He hears me. You know, Liz, when you told me about your change, at the time I was so wrapped up in my own troubles that I am just a horrible friend," cried Sydney. "Liz, I should have been there for you. I was so selfish, just concerned only about my life, my bad marriage, and I should have been there for you."

"Sydney, it is okay. This is the question that I had to answer when I was going through all that stuff with Tony. Rebecca did me like I am doing you. She posed this question to me. "Is God enough?"

"What do you mean, Liz, is God enough?"

"Is having God in your life enough to give you peace, joy and happiness? Even when you do not have a man nor a prospect of one in your life, Sydney?" Is God enough to let go the pain of your divorce? Is God enough to let go the hurt caused by Clarence? Is having God enough? Sydney, if you knew God, then He would be enough. Because nothing is greater than Him."

Sydney turned to Liz, "Right now, I really need to sit down, Liz." Both ladies sat on the sandy shore as the sound of the peaceful waves filled the air. Sydney dropped her head and cried. "God, please forgive me, I am so sorry, Liz, I am."

"Why are you saying you are sorry, Sydney?"

"Cause, Liz, I was a terrible friend when you were going through all that stuff with Tony. I was not there for you. And now, and now…,"

"Sydney, it is all right, stop crying, it is okay. Maybe that was exactly the way the Lord wanted it."

"No, I am your friend, and friends are to be there for one another no matter what. Look, right now all of you are here for me."

"Yes, yes, Sydney, we are friends, and yes, we are to be there to help one another, but at the time in my life the only person I needed was God. I knew what you were going through too. My goodness, Sydney, I understood, I had a wedding fall apart, but you had a marriage, kids, and your family fall apart. Trust me, I understood your struggle, and I never thought a minute that you did not love me or care for me."

"I do love you, Liz. I am so glad the Lord sent you here for me. I need His peace too. Liz, I need to know Him. Like you know Him. I need to answer your question. I do not know if he is enough. But I need Him to change my life like He changed yours. I need to say, Yes, God, You are enough, and You are all I need. I want to say that with all my heart."

"Then tell him that, Sydney, tell him that! He is right here standing with us. The Bible said where there are two or three gathered in His name that He is in the midst of them."

"Are you for real, Liz? Just telling Him that, that's it?"

"Yes, Sydney, it is that simple."

"And the Bible said that? Jesus is here with us right now? Right now? Standing right here?" asked Sydney.

"Yes, Sydney. Right here, so talk to Him. It is called prayer. I will pray with you, too." As tears flowed from her face, Sydney gave Him her heart, and she emptied her soul, and with anguish she released the deepness of her pains all in hope of His peace. As they prayed, the stars twinkled and the moonlight cascaded its reflection upon their faces. As they prayed, time became unimportant to them. As they worshipped, their surroundings became borderless; like children, they danced in the sand. As they danced in the sand, the other ladies curiously approached them and joined in the circle and danced too.

"Hey, what's all the dancing for? Why are you guys celebrating without us?" asked Belinda.

Sydney shouted, "Belinda, I got it! Sharon and Amanda, I got it! I got it! I got it, Liz, I got it! I can answer God's question.

"Hey, Sydney, what is it that you got and what was the question. What has happened?" asked Belinda as she pranced around."

"I got His peace I got His peace, and my answer is yes, God is my enough. I prayed to Him and he gave me His peace. Just like Liz said He would. I got it! I feel so light, like a bird, I got it!"

Belinda broke out into tears. "Oh, Sydney, I am so happy for you. I love that you got it. I love that God is your enough. It is so wonderful to see you so happy."

"Belinda, this is better than being happy. I feel so free, it is all gone, nothing is there, the heaviness, no anger, no hate, no depression. I mean, I got it. Sydney shouted, "God, you are enough for me, I want you and nobody else!"

"It's called joy," laughed Belinda. "It is the joy of the Lord. The Comforter has come into your very soul, Sydney, and He is your Helper, and He will teach you how to know God. He will do it."

With her hands raised to the sky, Sydney, yelled out, "Thank you, Belinda, thank you, God, thank you, Liz, thank you, Lord. Thank you, Lord!" As the ocean waves softly came to shore and the night wind warmly blew, they all danced together and celebrated Sydney's newfound peace.

Chapter Six
The Encounters

"Hey, Daniel, what is going on," screamed Clarence. "Where are my kids and Sydney? I have been calling her for the past three days and no answer."

"Man, I know you are not calling me asking me anything. Not after what you did. Are you crazy? I am not telling you anything else." Daniel hung up the phone. Daniel's phone rang again. "Man, what's wrong with you? I know this much, you better stop blowing up my phone. I have nothing to say to you after what you did to my sister, my nephew and niece. You say they are your kids? Really? Well, here is my advice to you, act like their father. Stop calling me. What? Uh, man, are you threatening me? I am telling you, you better erase that thought from your mind. Do not even think about it. Okay, go up there I will meet you there and when I see you, I am going to catch a case. But it will not matter because I am going to break one seriously off in you. What! Okay, you are still coming to the house. I will see you there. Yeah, you better bring whoever because I am going to put an end to your craziness. Daniel hung up the phone and talking to himself as he phoned his friend, Rico. 'I have had enough of this freak. I am putting an end to him bothering my sister and her kids.' "Hey Rico, get your boy Martinez, ya'll need to ride with me."

"Okay, Daniel we will be there in twenty minutes."

Liz goes to the beach early to relax and read her Bible. "Now, this is great," said Liz as she stretched back on her lounger. "Nothing is better than hearing the ocean waves, feeling the warmth of the sun, and sharing God's word with my girlfriends."

"Yes, this is so nice," said Amanda.

"Hey, I saw you from my window early this morning. What time did you get out here Liz, and who was that man you were talking to," asked Amanda.

"I got out here about five a.m. The guy said he is from next door." "Oh, is he with those guys who had the party," asked Amanda.

"No, he is from the house on the other side of us."

"What is his name, Liz?"

"I have forgotten it. He said he comes once a month to take care of the house for somebody. I do not remember. He kind of startled me this morning, but he seems nice. Listen, this morning I just wanted to enjoy sitting here doing nothing. All I could think about is that right about now if I were at work, I would be jumping up and running all day for Robert. So today, I jumped up and guess what? I did nothing," laughed Liz.

"Sydney," asked Liz, "who owns the beach house next to yours?"

"Oh, that house, it's awesome, right? It makes my house look like a garage," laughed Sydney.

"That family has been here as long as my family has. It is Mr. Grayson's house. He and my granddaddy were friends for years. I played with their grandchildren back in the day. But now I do not know if they ever come here. Who did you see? One of his grandsons?"

"Wait a minute, Sydney, are you talking about the Grayson and Grayson?"

"Yeah, Liz, have you heard of them?"

"Who have not, Sydney? They are the stars in the legal world. They are the crème de la crème. Every firm dreams of being like them."

Sydney stood up and looked to see if someone was there. "Uh, I do not believe I see anyone there. Did you see someone there, Liz?"

"Yeah, just the housekeeper the other day."

"Oh, I am not sure what time of year they come here, but if they do, I will take you over. Maybe you can meet one of them."

"You are kidding me! I would love to. Robert wouldn't believe it."

The ladies turned to see that the guys from next door had joined them on the beach. "Good morning, can we join you ladies?"

"Sure. I am sorry, I have forgotten your names," said Belinda.

"No problem. I am Joseph. This here is Brad, and this is the famous Ryan."

"Okay, do not listen to him. I am not famous," said Ryan.

"And guess what ladies," Joseph said happily, "we have our Bibles this time."

"Okay, good and welcome. I am Liz, this is Belinda, Rebecca, and,"

Brad quickly interrupted, Liz, "Wait, wait, I know you. Matthew Whitman's wife. Yes, yes, I kept telling these guys last night that you are the wife of Matthew Whitman. Now, tell them I am right."

"Man, Brad, chill out." said Joseph.

Brad turned and looked again at Rebecca. Quickly looked back at Joseph in excitement. "Hold on man, wait, am I right? You are Mrs. Whitman?"

Rebecca smiled, "Yes you are right. I am Matthew's wife."

"I told you man, hand it over. Hand it over right now." All the guys go into their pockets.

Rebecca looked. "Wait, you guys made a bet? Okay, it is not that serious," laughed Rebecca.

"Okay, now where was I before. Hey, this is Sydney, and the owner of our lovely beach house. Those two who are racing in the distance, I know you have met them already. By the way, how was your birthday party," asked Liz.

"It was all good. Everything was cool and your friends they were nice. We had a good time." said Ryan.

"Okay, now can we get back to the task at hand," asked Belinda?

"Hey, wait a minute!" shouted Myra. "Wait for Sam and me. We are coming. What is everyone doing," asked Myra.

"Bible study," said Belinda.

"What? Again," shouted Myra.

"Yeah, the guys will be joining us this morning. Are you two joining us for Bible study, too," asked Belinda.

"Yeah, I guess." said Myra.

"Good. Let us get started now that everyone is here. Let us turn to the book of what?"

"Sydney! Sydney! Come here right now," asked Daniel.

Sydney, quickly jumped up. "What are you doing here Daniel. What in the world is going on," Sydney, looked at everyone and apologized. "I am so sorry, please excuse me." As Sydney, and Daniel raced away, Liz jumped up and followed them.

"Okay, what is wrong Daniel? Why are you here? Why is Rico with you? Daniel Ford, Jr. what is going on," Sydney, walked up to Daniel, "Is Clarence coming here?"

"I am not sure. That nut case blew up my phone all morning. Acting all crazed about the fact that you will not answer his calls. I asked him to stop calling me asking about your whereabouts. This crazy man come talkin' about he is coming here because he wanted to talk to you and see his kids. I told him if he came, I would plant one so seriously deep in his butt, he would never recover. So, I called my boys and we got here as fast as we could to meet him if he comes."

"Daniel, you did not tell him where the kids are?"

Daniel shook his head, "No, no, Sis. I did not tell him anything. But today, it is on. Do you hear me? It is on."

"Daniel, how long ago did you talk with him," asked Liz.

"About an hour ago."

"Daniel, please stick around to see if he comes," asked Sydney.

"Okay. I will," said Daniel.

Liz turned to Sydney and Daniel, "I think he is frustrated and does not know what else to do but make you mad. He messed up by not taking the kids, and he does not know how to fix it."

"I do not know Liz, but I am not taking a chance. This cat is gone, I mean really gone. I told him, Man just be a good dad! How can he make all this fuss and say that he loves his kids? I do not understand him. But I know this much, its stops today. Sis, yes, I am just going to hang out here a while to make sure he does not show up. Sorry for busting in on you ladies at the beach."

"No, thanks, Daniel it's all right. Hey, there is breakfast in the house. You guys help yourself. Thanks again, Daniel. Love you."

"Love you too, Sis," said Daniel.

As Liz and Sydney, walked back to the beach to join the other ladies, Liz turned to Sydney, and asked, "Hey what are you going to do Sydney?"

"Liz, look at my face. I am not thinking about Clarence. I was freed of reacting to Clarence last night when God gave me His peace. If Clarence is foolish enough to come here, I will deal with it then. Other than that, right now we have our girlfriends and guests waiting on us to do a Bible study, and that is what we will do. After we finish, if Daniel and his boys have not eaten up all the food, we will feast and then take one of the longest naps on the beach that is possible. Now I do not know about you but that is my plan and none of it includes thinking, talking, or seeing Clarence. Are you with me, Liz?"

Liz, frozen in utter disbelief, "Yeah, I, uh, I am with you. I am totally with you," Liz walked and stared at Sydney.

"Liz," said Sydney, "stop staring, Liz."

"Sydney, are you sure you are okay," asked Liz.

"Yes, everything is just fine. Do not worry everything is okay," Liz and Sydney returned to the ladies and sat down to participate in the Bible study.

"Belinda, when I left, you said turn to where in our Bibles?" asked Sydney.

Belinda looked in astonishment at Liz, "Okay, you guys, you heard Sydney, let us get this Bible study started. Everyone turn to the book of Saint John, chapter 15."

"Liz, Liz," whispered Myra. "There are four books with the name John, which one is it?"

"Myra, the first one that is titled Saint. John."

"Which one did you say," asked Myra?

"The first one," said Belinda.

"Okay, where is the first one," asked Myra.

"Girl, ooh, the first one you come to," said Belinda.

"This should tell you ladies something when you cannot find the books of the Bible."

"Well, no, Belinda, it does not tell us anything, because we do not read the Bible."

As Belinda looked away from Myra, Liz quickly intervened. "Yes, you are right Myra, I am sorry. Let us keep turning, one more page. Here you go, it is right here," said Liz.

"Thanks, Liz," said Myra as she frowned at Belinda.

Teddy, the husband of Sharon and the cousin of Liz, called Daniel to check on the ladies. "Teddy, yeah man I remember you. Liz's cousin, right?"

"Yes," answered Teddy.

"Liz gave me your number if I needed to reach the ladies. Is everything okay? The fellas are a little concerned because none of the ladies are answering their phones."

"Hey, Teddy I am with them now. They are all fine. Right now they are all on the beach, but I am keeping a good eye on them."

"Okay, when you see my wife Sharon, please tell her to call me. Make sure you let her know it is not an emergency. Also, tell the rest of them to call their husbands too, so they can stop blowing up my phone."

"Okay," laughed Daniel, "Hey Teddy wait, I do not know which of the ladies have husbands."

"What's their names," asked Teddy

"Let me see. One is named, uh, Myra."

"Let me stop you right now. No man on earth would marry Myra," laughed Teddy.

"Man, Teddy that's cold."

"I know but do not let Sharon know I said that."

"The other lady, who I really hope is not married, she is fine as ever. Her name is Samantha."

"Who? Samantha."

"Uh, I do not know her. I have not heard Sharon or Liz talk about her. So, man you better be careful. Don't go making a move unless you are sure this girl does not have a man."

"Yeah, I know," laughed Daniel.

"Well, just tell my fine wife to call me. Later man," said Teddy.

"Later man," said Daniel.

Rebecca strolled along the beach shore with plans of sitting down to read her book and relax.

"Hello, Hello, wait up." asked Brad. "How are you, Rebecca?"

Rebecca, quickly turned around. "I am fine. Uh, wait, Brad, right?

"Yes. Rebecca, I stopped you to invite you ladies to dinner tonight. We are grilling and would love you all to join us."
"That is nice, Brad. However, I do not know because the others are not here. I will make sure I ask them when they come from the market."
Rebecca and Brad walked down to the beach shore as Rebecca prepared to sit down.
"Great. Hey, Rebecca, why didn't you go with them? Is the market not your thing?"
"Oh, no, I love the market. I just wanted to hang out on the beach and read for a while."
"Sounds good."
"I tell you Rebecca, this week is going by so fast. Are you guys leaving on Friday, too?"
"Yeah, we all fly out on Friday at noon."
"How long are you guys staying?"
"The same with us. Everyone is back to work on Monday."
"Well, I hope you make the best of your stay until then."
"Yes, that is what I am doing. Rebecca, the sounds of no phones, faxes, emails to answer, and all that stuff is all good."
"Yes," smiled Rebecca, "Well, thanks for the chat. Here is my spot. I am going to sink into my beach lounger, read, and relax. Thanks for the chat, Brad."
"Likewise, Rebecca. Hey, listen, just one more thing. I got some lemonade that is so good. It is the perfect drink to sip on while you enjoy your reading. My mom makes this lemonade, and it is the best in the world. I will bring some down to you."
"Ah, that's nice, but please do not go through all the trouble to bring it back down here. I am just fine, but thanks anyway."

Suddenly, Samantha appeared.
"Huh, well, what is this about," asked Samantha.
"Hey, Samantha, how are you," said Brad.
"The question is how are you doing, Brad. And what are you doing here?"
"Huh? Uh? Sam, well, anyway, Samantha, you are the perfect person to tell Rebecca what she would miss if she does not try my mom's lemonade. Help me to convince Rebecca to let me bring her some lemonade while she reads."
"Well, Brad, I believe you are wrong. I do not think I am the perfect one to convince Mrs. Rebecca Whitman to do anything. Perhaps, try one of her other friends. I got it Brad. The perfect idea. Why don't you ask her husband? Now, I know he could convince her to try your mom's lemonade."
Brad turned to Sam with a confused look. "Huh, okay, well, thanks for walking with me Rebecca. Hopefully, I will see you tonight."
"Thanks again for the invite, Brad. I will check with the others. Enjoy your day." said Rebecca.
"Well, well, is this not DeJa'Vu?"
"What? Get real Samantha."
"Up to your old tricks again? I wonder what Matthew would think if he saw his precious Rebecca talking so intimately with Brad. Did you forget you are married, Mrs. Whitman?"
Rebecca, looked firmly at Samantha.
"No, Samantha. The question is can you forget I am married?"
"Absolutely, yes," shouted Samantha.

"Then do so. DeJa'Vu? Nothing is further from the truth. Listen, I am the only one that needs to remember I am married. I have no interest in Brad, so there is no need for you to feel threatened."

"Threatened! Threatened! I am not threatened by you, Mrs. Whitman, and I have never been."

"Really? Well, the next time you see me talking to Brad then please act like you are not threatened."

Sam moved and stood directly in front of Rebecca blocking the sunlight. "I do not know who you think you are."

"Well, it is a good thing for your sake I know who I am. My suggestion to you is for you to truly find out who you are, and move on."

"Well, for your info I have moved on. It appears that it is you who have not, saying I am threatened and all."

"Goodbye, Samantha. I came out here for a purpose, and you are not that purpose. So good day to you."

Samantha, sharply turned and walked away.

Rebecca, laid back and took a deep breath and prayed out loud. "Lord I am trying but this girl is pushing it. I need your help because one more encounter like that and we all are going to look ugly. So, I am asking your help right now, Lord."

As Belinda approached, Samantha quickly walked pass her without speaking. Belinda looked back at Samantha, and said to Rebecca, "Do not tell me Samantha was talking nonsense again?"

"Belinda, I came out here to read and relax. I am not thinking about Brad or any man except my husband. This girl needs to move on and drop the foolishness. If she likes that guy, she had ample time to talk to him last night and this morning. Obviously, he is not interested and strangely that is my fault? Well, I asked her to move on, because I came here to relax and that is what I am going to do. I just prayed and asked for the Lord's help. So, I am fine. I am going to relax and read my book, Belinda."

"All righty then. I was just checking. I will see you at dinner in a little while," laughed Belinda.

"Okay," Rebecca, paused, "Hey Belinda, thanks for checking on me."

"You are welcome, Rebecca."

Liz rose early in the morning before all the other ladies to pray at the beach. Suddenly she is not alone.

"Good morning."

"Oh, good morning to you. Hey, you are from next door, right? I am sorry, I forgot your name."

"Yes, I am. My name is Ethan. You are up early too, Liz, right," asked Ethan.

"Yes, Liz. How nice that you remembered my name."

"Well, good morning Liz. I like to get up early and pray before I get my day going, too."

Liz moved in closer, "Are you a Christian?"

"Well, I like to say I am a Christ follower."

"Uh, what is the difference? Please forgive me, your name again."

"Ah, it's okay, Ethan."

"Okay, Ethan, what's the difference?"
"Well, I did not say that it was a difference, it's just my preference. Unfortunately, the meaning of the word Christian has drastically changed, and I wanted to distinguish myself as one who follows Christ. The nice thing is, that when I tell people that I am a Christ follower instead of a Christian, they want to know why, and this gives me a great opportunity to share Christ with them, like I am doing with you. So, how about you, are you a Christian?"
"That is interesting, Ethan. Yes, I am a Christian. I like to also get up early and pray. It is so beautiful here, and this is just a perfect place to sit and talk to God."
Ethan, looked around, "Yes, it is."
"You say you are the housekeeper of the house. How long have you been taking care of the house? I tell you what a privilege. It is one of the most awestruck beach houses here. What a privilege."
"I have been taking care of it for a while. I take it you are not from around here?"
"No, I am visiting with my friend and we are having a college girlfriend reunion."
"Sounds like fun."
"Yes, it is so great to see everyone. Just last night, one of my girlfriends on this very beach gave her heart to Jesus."
"Last night? Hey, that's awesome. So, I guess the week is going good for you?"
"Yes, it is. Thanks, Ethan, for sharing with me. See you around. I am going to pray."

"Yeah, thanks, too. Hey, later if you are free, I plan on doing some studying when I finish. I would love if you would join me," asked Ethan.

"Sounds good. We had Bible study yesterday, and the guys on the other side joined us. So, if we do it again, would you like to come?"

"I would love to come. I would love to but I am only free in the morning."

"Oh, I understand you have to take care of the house. Okay, then let us plan on praying and we can do Bible study in the morning. It's a date," laughed Liz.

"Right," laughed Ethan. "It is a date and don't be late, five a.m., right?"

"Yes, five a.m. right here."

"Nice talking with you, Ethan."

"Nice talking to you, Liz. I will see you tomorrow."

Liz prayed for a while, and enjoyed the cool morning ocean breeze. She returned to the house to find everyone enjoying breakfast. As Liz entered the house she yelled from the door.

"Hey, don't eat it all, save me some! What in the world has Chef Rio cooked up? I could smell it from the beach. It was hard to pray without thinking about food," laughed Liz.

"Hey, Liz, why didn't you wake me when you got up? I would have loved to pray with you," said Sydney.

"Me, too, Liz. Count me in next time you pray in the morning," said Belinda.

"Okay, Sydney, you, are getting up at five a.m. to pray?"

"Five a.m., who said anything about five a.m., it's eight a.m. You got up at five a.m.? No, no you are right. I thought maybe you got up at seven a.m. Wow, that is a long time, Liz. Did you pray the whole time?"

"Well, before I got started the housekeeper from next door came down to pray. I talked to him for a while. Did you know he is a Christian? Oh, no, not a Christian, let me say it right. He said he is a 'Christ follower'."

"What is a Christ follower," asked Amanda.

"Yeah," shouted Myra, "What is a Christ follower, and how is that different from any old Christian? People are always trying to make up new religions. Liz, come on tell us what a Christ follower is?"

"Well, before I was so rudely interrupted," Liz looked at Myra, "He said that a Christ Follower is a Christian who follows the teachings of Christ."

"Girl, nonsense, he is just a regular Christian. People are always making up new religions."

"Myra, Myra, are you a Christian?"

"Yes, I go to church. I may not be like all of you Liz, Rebecca, and the holier than thou, Belinda, but I am a Christian."

"Okay, Myra," asked Liz, "Being a Christian means what? I am not trying to put you on the spot, but truly tell me what it means to be a Christian to you."

"Well, Liz, since you asked, being a Christian means going to church. I believe in God and all the stuff Reverend Davis preaches. I give a little. I know I could do more, but nobody is perfect. Let me see, I follow the golden rule or the Bible. I am a good person, because I do not mess with anybody who do not mess with me. Now, I know maybe God is not done with me, but I am not as messed up as some other folks I know."

After Myra finished, silence filled the room and all the ladies' eyes were fastened on her.

"What's wrong with all of ya'll? Why are you guys looking at me like that? What? Okay, just say it. I am so sick of being criticized by all of you. So out with it," yelled Myra, "Out with it! Tell me how I am not a Christian! Tell me how I am going to hell! Just say it! I am so sick of all of you. Throughout college, it was pick on Myra. Myra you need to stop talking so much. Myra you need to do this and you need to do that," As tears flowed, Myra, yelled, "Out with it! Tell me how I am not a Christian, just say it!"

"Myra, I love you and you are not a Christian. Now, I have said it. Now you can stop yelling. If you would like, I would love to show you what the Bible says about what it means to be a Christian or Christ-like. It is your choice," said Liz.

"Liz, excuse me please," said Rebecca. As Samantha sat, Belinda, Amanda, and Sharon all stood to leave the table. Myra quickly turned to them and said, "No, do not leave. I really would like you all to stay. You know I do not know what it means to be a Christian. I do not know what to do. You see it is amazing to me to have you guys even as my friends. I know I do not fit in at all, but through it all, you all have still been my friends. I do not want to lose your friendship. I know I need to change, but I am not Liz. I am not smart like you. I am not Rebecca, I am not rich like you. I am not Belinda, who often reminds me, I do not have a husband or kids. I am not Sydney,

I do not have a house, let alone a beach house. Sometimes, I do not feel worthy enough to even be with you guys. Not that I would be missed or anything, but I did not want to come. I have painfully watched all of your lives take off and my life, which is going nowhere fast. I am 30-something and I have nothing but you guys. So, I put on and I try to just get along, but I see all of you are different. I see that all of you have some kind of thing with God that I do not have," Myra sat down and cried, "I do not know if God is my thing. All I know is I am tired of feeling less than." With everyone's eyes down cast, they all stood very still. Quietly, Liz pulled Myra beside her and prayed.

"Myra, the time is now. Yes, we are your friends, but as you see even having us as friends, is still not enough to feel good about yourself. The difference is what we have is God. All of us here have decided to get off the world's merry-go-round and give our hearts to Jesus, and you have watched each one of us do it. You say you have painfully watched our lives, then you will remember when I was left three days before I was to be married. You remember the hardship Rebecca had when she married Matthew. Also remember the challenge Belinda had when they wanted children. Now, you've seen Sydney reach for God to heal her heart after a broken marriage. It is not who we are, it is who He is, and He is God. Myra, admit it, you have been running from Him at every invitation. Remember, when you got into that car accident that landed you in the hospital. I prayed with you and you gave your life to Jesus, but Myra you refused to live for Him. You slowly started back, living like the old Myra. This time, Myra, you need to come to know God's love for you. It is in God's love where we find our worth. No man or friends can do that for you. Do you want to do it again, Myra?"

Myra slowly bowed her head and asked, "Liz, how do you know it will work this time?"

"Myra, I cannot answer that question. Only you can answer that question. Do you want it to work this time?"

"I do not know. I do not know if I want to give up guys and partying just to do what? I do not have a husband like Belinda and Rebecca, and"

Liz quickly interrupted, "Myra, what in the world are you talking about? I am single, too. I do not have a husband or kids, so how is it so different for you than me?"

"Well, you have a great job and stuff to take up your time."

"Stuff, what is the meaning of stuff, Myra?"

"Myra, listen to yourself, you are always making up excuses. You, Sydney, and I are all single. The question you need to answer, is God enough? Right now, you are talking about all the things you do not have and right before you is God offering you everything in Him. You need to make a choice. Listen, Myra the outcomes that you see and desire in all of our lives are the results of us loving and serving God and not of ourselves. Any good or beauty you see in our lives is because of Christ. So, I ask you is God enough?"

Myra lifted her head with tear-filled eyes and looked at all the ladies and softly answered, "I do not know Liz. I do not know."

"Well, Myra," asked Liz, "would you like us to all pray for you? Hopefully, afterwards you can figure out what you want to do."

Myra took a deep breath and said, "No, Liz, I have something to say first," Myra turned to Belinda and whispered, "Belinda, I will start with you first."

"Okay," Belinda said softly.

"I am sorry, would you please forgive me. I am sorry for always picking a fight with you. I guess I let my jealousy get the best of me. I am not jealous of you because you are married or have kids. My jealousy was because I feared that you, Belinda, would talk Liz out of being my friend. Liz is the only one who loved me whether I was good, bad, or ugly. I always wanted a close relationship with her like the one you have with her, Belinda. I fought with you. I know it was wrong and I am sorry."

Belinda stared at Myra and warmly responded, "Myra, please forgive me. I do not know what to say. I am sorry, too. I am the blame, too, because for years I have been very short with you. I was unaware of your feelings. Yes, I have to admit, I have questioned Liz why she is friends with you. But I have never tried to persuade her not to be your friend. I am sorry, Myra, that I gave you that impression."

Myra turned, walked to Rebecca, and softly spoke, "Rebecca, I am very sorry too. You have done nothing to me. Again, I was very jealous of you in all areas. Who would not be? But I felt angry at you because I felt you knew that Liz and I were very close before the wedding madness. We hung out, had dinner, and did so many things together. But after the wedding mess, Liz moved and all she talked about was what you and she were doing together. I was so hurt. I was wrong for inviting Samantha. I just wanted to get at you because I was hurt at your and Liz's relationship." Myra whispered, "Rebecca, I am sorry."

Tears flowed from Rebecca and she struggled to speak. She managed and gathered her words, "Myra, I accept your apology, but I am so hurt by what you did. Right now, I am so upset. I have not been honest with my husband. I have not told him that she is here. I have not ever done anything like that before. I simply wanted to spend time with all of you without any drama, but this puts me in such an uncomfortable place with Matthew. We do not keep secrets, especially when it involves something like this. I have not found a way to tell him that she is here. I was just hoping that the week went fine, and when I returned home Matthew would see that I am all right and will understand why I did not tell him. I forgive you Myra, but I am hurt by your actions. It was never my intentions to come between you and Liz. I am sorry that our relationship caused you pain."

Myra humbly responded, "No, Rebecca, it is all my fault. I am sorry for hurting you. After today, I will leave and ask Samantha to come with me."

"No," all the ladies said at once.

"Myra," said Sydney, "we do not want you to leave. Please, the week is almost over. Just maybe, this is what God wanted. Maybe this is what the weekend was all about. We say we are girlfriends forever, well, maybe it is time we deal with all the stuff openly and honestly. We should not hide our pain or our hurts."

Liz turned and walked over to Myra, "Why didn't you tell me I was hurting you? Friendship works both ways, Myra. Listen,

I love you Myra and you are right, but the things you have done to our friends is inexcusable. Hurting Belinda and this awful thing you did with Rebecca is the lowest. At this point Myra, I will have to question my friendship with you. I was not aware you were hurting others because you were hurt because you perceived they were interfering with our relationship. How could you do that? Are you aware how painful having Samantha here has been for Rebecca, who has never had a bad word to say about you? Myra, how could you? Do you understand how upset her husband will be when he finds out? Did you care that having her come would change a relaxing trip to a stressful week? I cannot do this right now." Liz turned away from Myra and said, "Belinda and Rebecca, I am so sorry that you had to endure such awful things at my expense. I do not have the words to say nor to express to you how sorry I am."

"Liz, Liz, please," interrupted Myra.

Liz turned and sharply responded, "Myra, Myra, please do not speak right now."

"Hey, guys could you please excuse me. I need a moment to gather myself. Right now, I really cannot do this."

Liz turned and stormed away.

"Liz," yelled Myra, "I am coming with you!"

Liz stopped, turned and walked back several steps, "Myra, right now, I need to be alone so please do not come. Thank you."

"Myra, come back. Give her space. She will be all right," said Belinda.

"I told her I am sorry, Belinda. What is wrong? Why does she not believe me?"
"She believes you Myra but she is hurt. She knows she has to forgive you. She is upset and too hurt to pray. Give her some time, Myra." Belinda looked at the ladies asking them to join hands and pray. "Ladies, let us pray and ask God to give us all peace."

Liz wandered down the shore of the beach and found a rock and perched herself upon it. She stared out at the ocean and listened as the waves crashed, she closed her eyes and cried. "Lord I am so angry. No, I am so mad. No, I am so hurt, please help me not be angry, mad, and hurt." As Liz prayed a voice came out of nowhere.
"Well, we are pretty far off from the house, aren't we?"
Liz, jumped and looked, "Ethan, Ethan is that you?"
"Yes, it is Liz, I see you remembered my name. What are you doing way out here by yourself? Oh, I am sorry. I see that you are upset. I do not mean to disturb, Liz."
"I am well, I came here to pray. I am well, but I need God's help." "Liz, may I pray with you?"
"Yes but wait, why are you here?" asked Liz.
"Well, I always take a late evening stroll before going home."
"Oh, I understand. Well, thank you. Yes, I would like it if you would pray with me. Ethan, first may I please tell you what happened."
Ethan, looked at Liz with a warm smile, "Sure Liz, please do."
Liz took a deep breath, "We were all gathered, and it actually started with your comment. You know when you told me that

you were a Christ follower instead of a Christian. Well, one of the ladies saw me talking to you and asked about our conversation. I told her that we had Bible study and prayer. Then one of my friends rudely interrupted and stated that you were making up a new religion. The long and short of it, we challenged her to what she thinks a Christian is, since she said she is a Christian. Well, again, the long story short, she finally confessed that she did not know what being a Christian means. I asked to pray with her, but she wanted to talk to all of us before we pray. Ethan, all of a sudden, Myra started on her own telling each person she was sorry for what she did to them. I was so excited. Ethan, you must understand she has never told anyone she was sorry about anything, even when she knows she is dead wrong. I knew the Lord was moving on her heart. But as she finished all the ones she had hurt, she did it because of me. Stating she hurt them because she did not want to lose our friendship or did not want them to interfere in our relationship. Ethan, one of the ladies, Rebecca, is so sweet and would never hurt a fly. She did something so awful to her. Now, not only did she ruin her week here by purposefully inviting a woman who stalked her and her husband for years, but she did not care about the repercussions behind such a thing. All she wanted was to get back at her. After my wedding mess, she saw Rebecca and my relationship grow closer. How ridiculous and unacceptable. Who has a friend like that? Why would I ever want to be friends with her if she is capable of doing such mean-spirited things? And now," Liz broke into tears and cried, "Ethan, I know that I have to forgive, which I already have. But I do not want to befriend her again." Liz exhaustively slid down off the rock and sat in the sand. “And you know Ethan, I cannot do that. Oh, Ethan, I am so sorry. I didn’t mean to dump this all on you.”

“No, no, Liz, it is okay. It is clear that her friendship is a special friendship.”

Liz, drew in the sand and said to Ethan, “Yes, we have been friends since college.”

“Well, Liz, the best of friends are capable of making mistakes.”

“Yes but it feels more than just a mistake. It feels like an evil doing to me. To purposefully set out to hurt someone is more than a mistake to me.”

“Yes, I agree that would be more than a mistake. but did I hear you say she was saying she was sorry for doing all those things?”

“Yes, but, I just, well, it’s no use. I just need to pray. Ethan, can we just pray now?”

“Yes, Liz if you like. I know many times it is hard for us to understand that in God there are no big or small sins. Just sins.”

Liz looked up at him, turned quickly and stared at the soon setting sun. “Do you think that is what it is? Because I say that what she did is more than a mistake that it was evildoing on her part? Which one is it, Ethan?”

“Well, no doubt that it’s not. But my point is when it comes to forgiveness, it does not matter to God whether it was a mistake or evildoing.” Ethan, smiled and said, “Liz, as a Christian or Christ follower, we all are commanded by Jesus to forgive and love our neighbor as ourselves. No matter the offense or how we classify them.”

Liz slowly looked up at Ethan, and put down her head in shame, and she released a deep sigh, "Yes, yes, Ethan, I hear you loud and clear. Now can we pray?"

"Yes, Liz, let us do that." As they prayed, the sound of the waves rush gently to the shoreline. When they finished, Liz asked, "Ethan, can we walk a little, please? Liz and Ethan, walked. Calmly Liz spoke, "Ethan, the air is quiet and so peaceful."

"Yes, it is. Liz when are you leaving," asked Ethan.

"Uh, in two more days."

"Have you enjoyed yourself?"

"It's unbelievable but I have Ethan. This is an amazing place, so peaceful and refreshing. You are so blessed to work here. I tell you, I would probably get fired if I worked here. It would be hard for me to stay off the beach. No, I take that back. With such a beautiful beach house, I would keep my job so I could have them both," laughed Liz.

"Ah, I see you are smiling now, Liz. It is good to see you are doing better."

"Yes, thank you, Ethan. You were God sent. I am so glad the Lord sent you my way. Thank you for listening to my story, and being such a great Christ follower to pray for me too," smiled Liz.

"My pleasure, Liz. I was hoping to run into you before you left."

"Well, you see, you did Ethan. God is in the business of answering prayers."

"Yes, he is Liz. By the way Liz, I never asked you what line of work you are in?"

"Well, I am an aspiring lawyer. Just before I came here, I had just taken the bar! So, this vacation is priceless for me. I work for my cousin who has his own firm in Houston. I am hoping when I get my results back, he will make me a partner, so please pray for that. My cousin Robert is quite the taskmaster, but I appreciate him. I know he wants the best for me. Ethan, I have worked hard these past seven years. I wanted to be really prepared to be a good lawyer. By the way, Ethan, my friend, Sydney, you know the one next door, tells me you work for the famous and prestigious law of Grayson & Grayson. The best law firm ever. Oh, my goodness, what is that like, Ethan, working for them?"

"Did you say, the most famous and prestigious law firm ever?"

"Yes, ever. I mean, most of my case studies were ones done by Grayson & Grayson. It is so funny, just wait until my cousin finds out that I was right next door to his champion of law firms."

"How do you think you did on the bar," asked Ethan.

"Well, I pray that I did well. I feel good about it. I studied for a year before taking it. My cousin was also a great help. Yep, I have hope against hope, Ethan."

"Well, I will stand in agreement with you on that, too."

"Hey, Ethan, you wanted to see me before I left. What is going on?"

"Yes, I did, Liz. I was wondering if you did not have plans with the ladies tonight and feel like a change of venue, perhaps you would like to have dinner with me tonight? Do you like Italian?"

"Yes, that sounds great. I love Italian food. It's a yes."

"Great, Liz. I know the perfect place. How about we meet up at six o'clock?"

"Yeah, six o'clock is good. Thanks, Ethan, for finding a great way to end the day."

"You are welcome. I am glad I was able to help, Liz. Okay, I will contact you and we will meet up."

As Liz strolled back to the house, she sees Rebecca and Belinda coming to greet her.

"Hey, Liz, are you all right," shouted Belinda.

"I am fine, just fine, ladies. I had my talk with the Lord and you will not guess what happened? While I was there, I ran into Ethan."

"Who," asked Belinda.

"Ethan. Remember the housekeeper from next door, Ethan? I told you about him."

"Okay, yes, I remember. This is the same guy that you have been doing Bible study with for the past couple days," asked Belinda.

"Well, he was walking along the beach and I ran into him. It was a God send. Unfortunately, I dumped all my stuff on the poor guy, but he listened and prayed with me. Then we just sat and talked. I tell you, it is really great to meet a real Christian guy, who loves the Lord. So, guess what ladies, I am going to dinner with him tonight."

"What," they yelled, "to dinner?" Liz, you barely know this man," said Rebecca.

"Yes, one of us should go with you," said Belinda.

“No, I will be fine. Ethan, is a real Christian and a gentleman. I will be all right. Plus, the restaurant is on the beach so it is fine. He is truly a sweetheart of a guy.”

Rebecca laughed and said, “Yes and it helps that he is so cute, too.”

All the ladies turned their heads and laughed.

With a shyness in her voice Liz said, “Okay, come on, it is not that kind of dinner. Ethan is such an easy guy to talk too. I think it will be fun after such a challenging time earlier.”

“What time are you going to dinner?”

“We are meeting up at six, so I need to get home and get dressed. By the way how is Myra,” asked Liz.

“She is fine,” said Rebecca. “We prayed with her and told her we will table this discussion until the morning at breakfast. I believe if we all get a good night sleep everyone should feel better. We needed to put some distance between what all happened today.”

“Yes, I think that is good. I talked with Ethan and he gave me some good advice about how God wants us to love one another. So, yeah, in the morning is good. Where is Myra now?”

“She and Samantha went off with Daniel and his friends. It is obvious that Daniel likes Sam.”

“Well, I hope Daniel knows what he is walking into,” laughed Liz.

“Hey, Rebecca, what is Liz getting all dolled up for?” asked Sydney.

“She is going on a date, but she said it is not a date. She is going out to dinner with the housekeeper next door.”

“With whom,” asked Sydney.

"She is going on a date," said Rebecca.
"Wait, I got that part. Who did you say she was going to dinner with?"
Rebecca looked curiously at Sydney, answering slowly, "With the housekeeper next door."
Sydney's eyes grew big and she motioned Rebecca to come to the balcony with her. Unable to control her laughter, Rebecca, moved to Sydney and whispered, "Okay, girl what's up?"
Sydney, holding her mouth, ran to the far part of the balcony and laughed, "Girl, I have known this family all of my life. I also have known their housekeeper for years, who so happens to be a lady by the name of Anna."
"What," shouted Rebecca.
Sydney, quickly said, "Shh, be quiet, Rebecca. I will tell you in a minute when Belinda join us too."
Belinda tiptoed over to the balcony to the others and whispered, "What is going on?"
"Rebecca, tell me what he looks likes," said Sydney.
"Well, he is tall, slender built. He is handsome."
"Well, does he have curly hair or a bald head?"
"He has curly hair."
"Ethan," laughed, Sydney, "the little master mind, Ethan Grayson, III."
"What," yelled Rebecca! "Grayson & Grayson." Yes, he is one of the sons of the law firm!"
"In the flesh. I am going to get him. Just wait until I see him," said Sydney.
Liz suddenly appears. "Hey what are you guys talking about? Tell who what about what," asked Liz.

Sydney quickly changed the conversation. "Oh, girl, now you must look stunning for your nondate."

Liz shook her head, "Listen, I already told you, we are just hanging out. Okay, ladies, I will be back. I will tell you all about it when I come home, so wait up."

"Wait, Liz, let me get this right. You just finished taking the bar, plan on being a lawyer and a partner at Robert's law firm, and you are eager to go out on a date with a housekeeper? Let me get this straight, girlfriend, and that is all right with you?"

Liz shook her head at Sydney, and said, "My, my Sydney, I never thought the day would come when you sound like Myra." Liz turned to the other ladies and asked, "Did you guys hear her? Sydney, I cannot believe you said that."

Amanda looked at Liz with surprise and said, "Come to think about it Liz, I am surprised too."

"Well, you see Liz we are all surprised at you. Again, are you sure you want to go on a date with a housekeeper?"

"Okay, that is it. All of you guys are just pitiful. Did you not hear me when I told you how much he helped me with the whole Myra stuff? Ethan listened and prayed with me. He is truly a nice guy. I told you he is a Christian or he calls himself a Christ follower," smiled Liz, "You guys cannot be serious? Well, it will not work. I will not allow you all to spoil my soon to be great time, with a great guy, who so happens to be a housekeeper. So goodbye ladies and now do not wait up for me," Liz turned to walk out of the door.

All the ladies laughed, "Ah, Liz," said Sydney, "we are all just messing with you. We are just kidding girl."

Liz turned and laughed. "Okay, that is better. Now you ladies can wait up for me and I will talk to you when I get home.

"Yeah, Liz, nonetheless remember he is a housekeeper," laughed Sydney.

Liz walked to the door and looked back and laughed as the ladies' laughter filled the kitchen.

"I am not listening," said Liz as she went out of the door waving bye to the ladies.

"Okay, Sydney, she is gone. Now give us the scoop," said Belinda.

"Okay, two months ago I came to the house to get things ready. I had to also meet Chef Rio, the housekeeper, and the masseuse. While I was there, Ethan, saw me and came over. He was getting his house ready, too."

"What! That is his house," asked Belinda.

"Yes, girl. We met outside and I told him all of you were coming here. I showed him pictures of you guys, and immediately Ethan was interested in Liz. Especially, when I told him she was like him, very religious. He wanted to know everything about her. Girl, Ethan kept me here for about two hours asking me questions about Liz."

"So, he knows about her," asked Rebecca.

"Well, yeah," said Sydney.

"Everything," asked Rebecca.

"Well, no, I... I do not think everything. I do not know. Because about a week later, Ethan called me and girl, he had done a complete search on her."

"What! Do you think if she finds out that she will be all right with all of that," asked Rebecca.

"There is a possibility that initially she may not be okay with knowing how he came to know her. But perhaps afterwards, finding out that he is a lawyer too, maybe she would think it is flattering," said Sydney apprehensively.

"Yeah, I think you are right, Rebecca."

Belinda fell into the sofa and just laughed, "So Miss Control is out of control, and being had by a make-believe housekeeper millionaire. I tell you it does not get any better than this."

All the ladies broke out in laughter.

"Okay, now you have to tell us about him. We need to know if Mr. Wonderful is wonderful." said Rebecca.

"Girl, Ethan, like Liz said is a very nice guy. I have known him all my life. He is truly like a brother to me. When we were little, we shared every summer here with our folks. His grandfather and mine where the best of friends. Ethan, comes from a good family."

"Okay, then answer the million-dollar question, why is he still on the market? What is wrong with him," asked Belinda.

"Girl, nothing is wrong with Ethan. From what I know, he went off to school and got very involved in some religious stuff. Next thing I knew he totally changed from his earlier days in college. By the time he got to law school he was different, more mature, and a very serious person. So, I guess, he just wanted the same type of woman. His family is also very religious, so I can imagine they would want him to find the same kind of a lady. Oh, yeah, also because of all the wealth left to him and his brother from their father and grandfather, I would be cautious too. Ethan, is a great guy. Like I said, like a brother to me."

"Well, that's one brother you should have tried to get yourself," laughed Belinda."

"Girl, no! When I say, he is like a brother, I mean like a brother," laughed Sydney.

"It would be great if he and Liz hit it off. We have to do whatever we can to help this happen. This is great. They are perfect for each other. Let us take a little trip and spy on them," said Sydney.

"Yes, let us do that," said Rebecca.

By this time Ethan and Liz were at the restaurant. "Wow, you look nice tonight Liz," said Ethan.

"Thank you, Ethan. You too look great," said Liz.

"Ethan, this is an amazing restaurant, it has such an old-world charm."

Ethan looked around, "Yes, Liz it is my favorite place. Wait until you taste the food, and the service is amazing too. But this place has something you must see."

"Do you come here often? At least once while the house is open. The chef is the best on the beach."

"I love it. It's such a warm place. The strange thing, and you will not believe this, Ethan, but Italian food is my favorite."

"Good, then I am glad, Liz, I made a great choice."

"Sir, your table is ready."

"Oh, my goodness, this is so beautiful. Look at this view. This is breathtaking. Ethan, this is absolutely beautiful. Look at the sunset,"

"Yes, Liz, we can watch the sunset as we are having dinner.

"Excellent." said Liz.

"Yes, my thoughts exactly. What a view." said Ethan.

"Oh, yes, Ethan. Such a beautiful place for dinner. Everything is excellent. Thanks so much for inviting me. This has made my day. No, actually this has made my trip."

As the sunset, Liz got lost in the evening. She and Ethan shared heart-warming exchanges of laughter and great food. Minutes slipped into hours as the dusk faded away and unwrapped a starlit sky. With the final course is on the table, Liz looked and gazed into Ethan's eyes and for the first time tonight she noticed how beautiful they are and the warmness of his smile. She slowly rested on the back of her chair unable to stop the floodgates of thoughts rushing in. She thought to herself, "what in the world is going on with you girl? Look at you, why on earth are you allowing yourself to feel something for this man? But everything is so perfect, help God! What is happening? Okay, Liz, get yourself under control? Calm down. Your emotions are raging inside. Okay, girl, take a deep breath. I know, go to the restroom, and get yourself together. "Excuse me, Ethan, I need to go to the ladies' room."

Ethan, stood up. "Sure, Liz, it is over to your left."

"Thanks." Liz raced off to the restroom and ran into the stall. She thought to herself, "What do I do? I got to settle down. This is not a date. It's just two friends getting to know each other, and nothing more. Oh, God please help me. I know I will call Rebecca. No, no, they will just tease me about going out with him. I cannot tell them that I am having feelings for him. Lord, help me. I do not want it to show. Please put me back in the mode I was in before I looked in his beautiful brown eyes and enjoyed his warm smile. Please, Lord, help me. Okay, God now is not the time to be silent. It is not funny, speak now. Okay, have it your way, but I asked you to help me. Here I go out there again. Give me strength."

"Sorry, for the delay, Ethan. Well, Ethan, I cannot tell you how much I have enjoyed tonight. It was perfect. Thank you so much for inviting me. Everything was perfect and I truly enjoyed everything."

"No, Liz, truly the pleasure was all mine. I am so glad to hear that you truly enjoyed yourself and had a great time. The food is the best, right?"

"Oh, yes. Right, the best. But that view is overwhelming to take in."

"I know, it is great. Hey, just a few minutes more. Let us go out and enjoy it before we leave."

"Oh, …uh."

Ethan, looked at Liz, "Liz, is there something wrong?"

"Oh, no...Okay, just a little while before we go."

"Okay, follow me." Liz slowly walked to the balcony, all the while she is talking to God. God! God! Liz screamed, I am not playing, help. You see it is a starlit sky. Look, God, it's not funny.

"Hey, Liz!"

"Hey, look Ethan, it's my friends. Hey guys what are you doing here?" asked Liz.

"Hey, Ethan, how are you?"

"Hey, ladies, how are you? Funny meeting you here."

"Yeah, we just decided to take a nice stroll on the beach and wow, we ran into you guys," said Sydney.

Sydney smiled and asked, "Ethan, how was dinner?"

"Uh, it was very nice."

"Yes, it was very nice." Liz quickly answered too.

"Really, Liz, well, it appeared that you had a good time," said Rebecca.

"Ah...I mean, I did Rebecca."

"Well, ladies, I know when I am outnumbered. If it is okay, Liz, I will leave you with your friends."

"Oh, yeah that's fine, if you do not mind, Ethan?"

"No problem, I will see you in the morning for Bible study.

"Okay. Again, I had a great time. Thanks for joining me."

"No, thank you Ethan. I really enjoyed it. See you in the morning. Good night."

Belinda grabbed Liz by the hand, "Look at me, let me look in your eyes because the eyes do not lie. Do not tell me...yep...it is too late ladies. One date and she has fallen for the housekeeper."

"What! Let me look. "Liz, you are not serious. He is a housekeeper. Are you falling for this guy?"

"Wait, guys, listen, let me sit down. Come on guys, give me a minute. I truly do not know what happened. We were having a great time. Then all of a sudden, I looked at his eyes and his warm smile and then it happened. I started to have these feelings for him. I did not try. I do not know what is going on. You guys know ever since the ordeal with Tony, I have worked so hard to shield myself against acting impulsively. For the past seven years, I have had several dates and seen lots of good-looking guys. But nothing. When I say nothing. I mean nothing. Perhaps, it is this place that has caused me to relax my guards. I do not know what is going on. And yes, you are right

Belinda he is a housekeeper. But he is so nice, and I so enjoyed being with him tonight. I saw myself falling for him and I prayed, and you guys show up."

"Girl what are you talking about," asked Belinda.

The first time I felt something, I got up and ran to the ladies' room. I could not believe it myself. I thought, oh, my goodness, I cannot let this man know I have feelings for him, especially since all he has been is a complete gentleman. I asked myself, girl what is wrong with you? You have to get yourself together. I prayed to God to help me. So, when I got back to the table, which by the way I was gone too long, Ethan asked me to take a stroll on the beach. I lost it inside. I screamed at God to help me and here you are. Prayer works ladies, prayer works."

"Well, Liz, did you sense that Ethan was interested in you," asked Sydney.

Liz stared and took a deep breath, "Well, this was what disturbed me a little. I sensed that Ethan planned the entire dinner to attract me. Everything was done to my taste. How could that be? It seemed strange, like Ethan knew me more than just our couple of Bible studies or brief conversations on the beach. Why was I so relaxed with him? I just do not know what happened you guys."

"Well, again Liz, what are you going to do," asked Belinda.

"I really do not know. Well, for right now, go home, take a long bath, and pray to God. My goodness I have Bible study in the morning with him. I know how you guys can help me. Please get up with me and come down, so I will not feel so awkward."

"I am not sure girl. That is too early for me," said Amanda.

"Ah, Liz, that is the last day I can sleep in," said Sydney.

"Girl, I cannot promise." said Belinda.

"Come on guys, just try. This is really important to me. I really need you guys," begged Liz.

"Girl, Liz, stop bugging. We said we will try," laughed Belinda. Sydney's phone rang. She looked down at it and saw it was Ethan. Sydney quickly answered the phone and leaves the room. "Well, hello Mr. Wonderful or Mr. Housekeeper, which do you prefer," laughed Sydney."

"Neither. Do not be funny, Sydney. "You just so happened to be on the beach at the same time? Come on, Sydney, you guys were spying on us. Okay, I know you ladies talk, what did she say about me? Is she the least bit interested in me?"

"Well, yes and yes."

"Come on, Sydney, I am serious. What did she say? How do you know that she is interested in me? Stop playing games and just tell me."

"First, tell me this. Are you serious about a relationship with her?"

"Yes, especially after dinner. She is so awesome. I had a hard time keeping it together. I do not know what I am going to do at Bible study in the morning. Sydney, how can I conceal how I feel about her. I need to know how she feels about tonight. Come on. Was she the least bit interested? What did she say? Sydney, you are doing this on purpose, come on and answer me."

"I did answer you, Ethan. I said, 'yes and yes,' Ethan. Yes, she talked about you while we were walking on the beach. And yes, she is very interested in you, too."

"What! Yes! Great!" shouted Ethan.

"But Ethan, you, have one big problem. Liz, thinks you are a housekeeper. How in the world are you going to fix that?"

"I know. You have to know that was not part of my plan. The first time I saw her on the beach I was not prepared to be so taken back. She is beautiful. My heart just raced, so when she asked me what I was doing. I told her I was taking care of the house. She replied, 'Okay, you are the housekeeper,' I just hurried up and said yes, because I did not want her to know who I was. Well, I am the keeper of the house even though I am not the housekeeper. Each day, I struggled with how I am going to tell her who I am. Then two days ago, she went on this spill about how pretty the house was and how great our law firm is, I lost my guts. Sydney, what should I do?"

"Oh, no my brother, or should I call you Mr. Housekeeper, a.k.a. Mr. Ethan Grayson III. You are on your own. You got yourself in this, so figure it out on your own. I have given you more than enough information."

"Sydney, did you forget? I am a lawyer remember. You have said nothing."

"Okay, okay, listen, Ethan, normally we do not give out this information. This is usually strictly kept between us ladies. But yes, you made a great impression on her. She is going nuts because she is interested in you too. I must say, you did a great job impressing her at dinner. So yes, she is very interested in you. But remember again, she thinks you are a housekeeper."

"She is struggling with being interested in a housekeeper?"

"Well, once I found out that she was talking about you. Me and my girls purposefully teased her about you. She was very protective of you. She got at us for judging you by what you do. Because she looked at you as a friend. Now, that she is just as interested in you, I know she is struggling with it. Do not get me wrong, Liz is the sweetest person. The thing that has captured her is that you love God. That is why she is struggling. She sees how much you love God, Ethan. Liz, is torn between common sense and what make sense to her. This is a new place for her. When I tell you this girl runs from being in a relationship. This is such a God thing that just happened. She is struggling right now, not so much that you are the housekeeper, but that she is interested in you so quickly. She questioned her own feelings. Now, right now, Ethan, she really does not know how you feel. It is funny to see her so nervous, but so delightful at the same time. So, you have done a good job concealing your feelings, but you got one day left and what are you going to do? I suggest you go and pray too. All ladies love the rags to riches story, but Liz, is different, she may be a little put back by the whole ordeal, but there is a possibility she may look at it as kind of deceptive."

"What do you mean? I never set out to deceive her, Sydney."

"I know Liz is a very serious person, too. And she does not know you that well. So, she could view what you did as a test or something. She may view it as you testing to see if she wanted you if you were not wealthy or something. Now, that is not Liz. She is the best of the best. But she thinks deep, and there is a possibility she may be a little taken back."

"Okay, Sydney, that's when I will need your help."

"What...uh...help? No. If that happens, she will talk to you. You have to tell her the truth. You know the truth. "Sydney, she is so important to me. You have to help me. I need you."

"Okay, Ethan, I will help you on one condition."

"Anything Sydney, anything."

"That you never break her heart. If you are not serious about her, then stop right now. But if you break her heart, I promise you I will never speak to you again, ever."

"Sydney, why would you make me promise that? I am not that kind of person and you know that. Right now, I truly care for her. I hope she feels the same. I am looking for a wife. I am ready to have a family. I have thought hard about this. The only way it would happen is if she does not want it to happen. My intentions from the start were to get to know her this week, and for her to get to know me. Sydney, I want a serious relationship. Not some fling. You know I am not that kind of guy. I promise if I can capture her heart, I will never break her heart," said Ethan.

"Well, you already hit a home run, Ethan. You have captured her heart already. Good night, my friend."

"Thanks, Sydney, good night to you."

"Wait I got one more thing. Liz has begged Rebecca to come to Bible study with her in the morning because she is afraid of how she will act around you now that she is attracted to you. Rebecca will come, but she will leave to go to the ladies' room and never return, so work your stuff."

"Tell Rebecca, thanks too, this means so much to me, Sydney."

"Yeah, yeah. Just do not blow it Mr. Housekeeper," laughed Sydney.

The next morning Liz is waking up the others to come with her to the beach for Bible study with Ethan. Liz goes in the room where Belinda and Rebecca is sleeping.

"Hey, Belinda. Belinda come on, get up," whispered Liz.

Belinda turned over, "Liz, no, I cannot do it," said Rebecca.

"Rebecca, Rebecca, come on. I really need one of you to come with me, wake up."

"Liz, please I am so sleepy. It is just Bible study, what could possibly happen?"

"Listen, I prayed last night and nothing changed. I do not want to go down there by myself. Come on, Rebecca."

"Oh, okay, Liz. This is the last day that I can sleep in late. Okay, Liz, but you owe me big and I mean big."

"Thanks so much, Rebecca."

"Will you two be quiet and get out. This is my last day I have to sleep in," screamed Belinda.

"Okay, Rebecca, here is the plan. You sit between him and I. This way I do not have to look directly at him."

"Liz, okay. Enough. Did you ever think he may like you, too?"

"Rebecca, what in the world are you saying? Listen, we had a great time last night at dinner. I am the one who got hooked. He was just himself. So, I am the one that has to keep it together."

"Okay, Rebecca. Look he is out there, let us go."

"Liz, what do you think about the fact that he is a housekeeper and you will be a lawyer?"

"I know. I said to myself, girl what are you doing? Why are you falling for him? I know he is a housekeeper, but I guess, I do not know. I will not stop being his friend because he is a housekeeper. By the way, look at the house he has to keep. They must see something more in him to trust him to manage their home. Rebecca, why did you have to ask me that? It's too distracting."

"Distracting how," asked Rebecca.

As the two slowly approached the beach, Liz, answered Rebecca's question. "Distracting, because what I see in him is how much he loves God. I love talking to him. This is what I feel is my connection. So, when you ask me about him being a housekeeper, it is just a distraction from who he really is. He is such an awesome man. Okay, enough, we are here."

"Good morning, ladies," said Ethan.

"Good morning," sang Rebecca." Liz turned and looked at her in shock.

"Ah, good morning, I didn't know you could sing Rebecca."

"Well, it's our last morning here, and I just wanted to do something different."

"Well, let us get started, ladies. I may have to leave you a little early, I have some things I need to take care of," said Ethan.

As the three shared, the sun slowly peaks out and the ocean waves gently touched their feet. Rebecca jumped up. "Excuse me please, I am sorry, but I must go to the ladies' room."

"Right now? Can it wait? Rebecca, we are almost finished," asked Liz.

"I am afraid not. Hey continue on. You know how it is when you got to go, you got to go," Rebecca ran to the beach house.

"Liz, is everything all right? You seem different?"

"Ah, Ethan, everything is just fine. Why? What do you see?"

"Well, nothing. Well, I thought since this is your last day here and since you talked so much about the house, would you like to see inside?"

Liz jumped up. "Are you kidding me? Can we? I mean, is it okay? You will not get in any trouble?"

"No, no it is okay."

"Oh, my goodness, Ethan." In Liz excitement, she grabbed Ethan and hugged him. "Oh, I am so sorry. I got carried away. It's just I have been wanting to see it, but I did not have the heart to ask."

"Well, now that you have the opportunity, Liz. I am so delighted."

"Well, I am so happy you are delighted," said Liz.

"Yes, you see I wanted to rub in it my cousin Robert's face that I saw the house. He is always talking about Grayson & Grayson this and that. Just wait until he finds out. Thanks, so much Ethan, you have made my day! Just wait until Robert finds out! He will be so jealous."

"Well, if you like Liz, you can take pictures too."

"What! Yes! Okay, this is great."

"Okay, are you ready, Liz?"

"Right now?"

"Yes, right now, Liz."

"Wait, let me see if I have my phone. Ah, wait, I need it to take pictures. Oh, there it is. I have it. Let us go, Ethan."

"Ethan, they must trust you very much to look after such a great house?"

"Yeah, I think they do."

"What all do you do?"

"I do everything."

"My, that's a lot. When will they visit?"
"Oh, I never know. One of them could be here now."
Liz stopped Ethan and pulled him by the hand away from the house. "No, no. I do not want to go if anyone is there. I thought the house was empty."
"Well, it was when I left, but someone could have come while I was at the beach."
"Well, how will you know, Ethan? And what will they think of you bringing a stranger into their home? Are you sure this is okay?"
"Okay, Liz, slow down. I will know once we get past the security gate. No, they do not mind me bringing a friend into the house. And yes, again it is okay that you come. Now can we go in?"
Liz, whispered, "Ethan, is anyone home?"
Ethan laughed, "Liz, why are you whispering? Relax it's okay, you are fine."
"Oh, my Ethan, this is beautiful. How could you possibly manage all of this? Everything is so magnificent. Is this a portrait of Mr. Grayson?"
"Yes, it is."
"Oh, my goodness, this house has a library. Now here is where I want to take pictures."
"Oh, wow, look at these. I know they must have worked on countless of cases right here. Okay, come on Ethan, let's take a picture right here by the desk."
"Oh, by the desk? Okay, Liz, by the desk."
"Come on, Ethan. Okay, I got to get the desk in the background. Okay, stand next to me. Okay, good. Here we go.

Smile! Got it. Yes, Ethan these look great. Now, let's take one next to these books. Okay, ready?"

"Ready. You look amazing, Liz."

"Come on, Ethan just take the picture."

"Okay, done."

"Let me see, Ethan. Good. Now, uh, let's,"

"Liz, come over here let me show you this before you take another picture," Liz moved slowly to the doors as she opened them, and awed.

"Ethan, look at this view. I do not have words. It is so beautiful. Ethan, may I sit?"

"Please do, Liz. From here you can see the entire beach." Liz, still stunned and speechless, she whispered, "Look that is where we had Bible study this morning. Oh, Ethan, it is something to behold. Can we sit for a minute?"

"Yes, Liz, I would love it if we would sit for a minute. I have something to tell you."

Liz, still dazed by everything, sighed with a deep breath as she answered, "Ethan, what is it?"

"Liz, I do not want to hide my feelings from you any longer. Liz, I am very interested in seeing you. I have very strong feelings for you, and I want more than just a friendship."

Liz, immediately stood up and moved to the stone railing. "Ethan, uh, you have strong feelings for me? You, uh, you, uh you do not really know me that well. How do you know that you have strong feelings for me?"

"Liz, I will answer that if you tell me if you feel anything for me at all. Do you Liz? Do you feel anything for me at all, am I just a friend only? Please be honest with me Liz."

Liz walked to the other side of the railing and gazed out to the ocean, closed her eyes, and slowly released each breath. "Ethan, I do have feelings for you. And yes, they are more than a friend. But I am not sure why it happened so soon. I really do not know you, but I feel like I do. I am so confused about this whole thing. One minute, we are having Bible study, then dinner, and now everything has changed. I am not sure how all of this happened so fast."

"Liz I may know why some things are happening so fast."

"What are you talking about Ethan?"

"First, thank you for being so honest with me. I am so glad that you have feelings for me more than just being a friend. I know today so many folks are so guarded. But Liz, now I need to know your heart before I go on. Okay, I need you to hear me out please."

"Uh, Ethan, what's going on? I am getting a little uncomfortable now. Why are you asking me to hear you out, Ethan?"

"Liz, Liz, please, come over here, and sit down. Just sit down, no need to be alarmed. Everything is fine. Listen, I asked you to be honest with me, and thank you for doing that. Now, I want to be honest with you.

Okay." Liz looked nervously at him, "Okay, Ethan. What is this about?"

"Liz, I want to tell you first, I am very interested in having a relationship with you. I know you do not know me well, but I want us to get an opportunity to do that. The reason why I say I may know why things are happening so fast! Is because this is your last day here. I really wanted you to know before you leave how I felt about you. Now, I am not trying to rush you into anything. I did not want to lose this opportunity to tell you. Liz, by rule I am not an impulsive person. I really think long and hard about having a relationship. I am not just looking for a girlfriend. I want more. But I know ultimately, it is up to you. Listen, I love the Bible studies we had, it gave me a chance to see the woman of God you are. And I must say, I love that. Last night at dinner, well, I, it was so hard to contain my feelings for you. I thought you saw right through me. Liz, I know this is a lot, and I am not trying to overwhelm you. I just wanted to tell you how strongly my feelings are for you. So what I am about to say to you I want you to calmly think about it. Liz, I…

Suddenly, out of the library a woman's voice called out, "Ethan, Ethan, where are you? Walter said you were in the library but you are not here."

"Oh, hello. Hello, here you are. She leaned over and kissed him. I have missed you son. It has been a month. Now you know that is too long between visits for me. Oh, do not tell me, is this Liz?"

"Oh, hello, mother."

"Son, where are your manners?"

"Good morning my dear. My name is Natalie Grayson. It is so nice to meet you." Liz, looked confusingly at Ethan, "Good morning, Mrs. Grayson, it is so nice to meet you, too."

"Oh, please call me Natalie."

"Now, tell me this. Liz, has my son been a perfect gentleman. I want to know. Hurry and tell me before his father come, in here. Oops, too late."

"Ethan, there you are son. Well, good morning to you two. Hello, my dear, I am Ethan's father, Benjamin Grayson II, but you can call me Ben. How are you? Now tell me, has my son been a perfect gentleman?"

Liz turned, took a deep breath and said, "Your son, Ethan, has been a perfect gentleman. I was just telling him I am sorry, but I have an urgent matter I need to tend to. I am so sorry, but thank you for allowing me to see your lovely home. But I really must go and take care of things."

"Oh, yes. Well, we understand. Will you be joining us for dinner? We heard this is your last night. So, we flew in to meet you before you go. We hope you can make it."

"Uh, I, may I please let you know?"

"Sure, no problem, the day is early. We will talk later."

"Goodbye and again you have a lovely home and thank you for allowing me to see it, and thank you for the lovely dinner invitation."

"Mom, Dad, let me walk Liz to the door."

"Okay, nice meeting you," Liz swiftly walked out of the library, out the door, and down the beach.

"Liz, wait," called Ethan, I can explain. Liz, if you would just listen. I can explain. Just wait one minute and let me explain. Liz, do not go to the beach, my parents can see you."

Liz, stopped turned and swiftly walked into the cabana. "How could you," Yelled Liz. "How could you? Why didn't you tell me? You know I really do not want to know. I think I know why. Well, Ethan, I hope your little plan worked."

"What plan? Liz, calm down and please let me explain."

"Oh, is this your plan? The plan of if you played a poor housekeeper, will she want me? The plan, where you find out if I would want you if you had money or not. That plan, Ethan! Why go to all the trouble, just do whatever one does who is rich? Well, I cannot say everyone, my friend Rebecca, do not have one. But you know what to do, you are a lawyer, do a pre-nup, right?"

"Liz, listen, I had no such plan. If you would just calm down, I can explain. I know all of this caught you off guard."

"All of this? Off guard?" yelled Liz, "How would you feel if you found out I am some kind of mass murder or something? How would you feel, Ethan?"

"Well, you are not. I already checked you out."

"What? What do you mean you already checked me out? Wait a minute. When did you check me out? What in the world."

"Liz, please just sit and just let me explain. Please give me at least thirty minutes and I can explain myself."

"Ten minutes, Ethan, you have ten minutes. I made a complete fool out of myself back there with your parents. Your parents!" Liz yelled, "Here I am thinking how much I am going to rub this in Robert's face about going to the house. Ethan, I ran directly into your parents. Oh, my goodness, they said they flew in to meet me. Oh, I just cannot believe this is happening to me. They must think I am nuts, the way I responded Ethan, how could you do that to me?"

"Actually Liz, you handled yourself remarkably well. I was impressed. You are quick on your feet."

"Ethan, do you really want to see how quick I am on my feet. Now you have five minutes."

"No, Liz. Okay, five minutes." Ethan, took a deep breath and poured out his heart to Liz.

"Belinda, have you seen Liz," asked Rebecca.
"Oh, yeah she's on the beach. Wait, Rebecca, weren't you with her this morning?"
"Yeah, but I left her and Ethan on the beach about an hour ago." Rebecca goes to the kitchen window to look for Liz on the beach. "No, I do not see her, Belinda." Rebecca, walked outside to the deck. "Belinda she is not out there."
"Maybe she went for a walk or something. She is all right. She should be back soon. She knows we have to get ready to pack and stuff. I have truly enjoyed this reunion with you guys. How about you Rebecca? Rebecca?"
Belinda goes to the deck to see where Rebecca has gone to. Rebecca runs down to the beach to find out why Liz is upset.
"Sydney, come quick. What is going on? Sydney, come quick! Something is going on with Liz," yelled Belinda.
"Where is everyone?"
"Down by the beach," said Sydney. Come fast something is wrong with Liz. What in the world is going on? Now, Rebecca, is crying too."
Belinda ran to the beach. "What is wrong, Liz? What is wrong, Rebecca? Where have you been, Liz? What has happened? Where is Ethan?"
"Belinda, Belinda slow down," as Rebecca, cried and laughed.
"What has happened," screamed Sydney. I'm coming. What is going on? Where is Ethan? What's happened? Liz, are you okay? Why is everyone crying?"

"Calm down, Sydney," laughed Belinda as she wiped her tears.
"Okay, will someone please tell me what is going on?"
"Sydney," said Liz, "I am just fine. I just got a little overwhelmed, but I am fine now. Let's go to the house and talk. First, Ethan told me everything. So as of today, my friendship with all of you ends after this conversation. All the ladies looked at Liz, and then burst out in laughter!"
"Got you! Elizabeth Irene Marshall has been had! Liz tell us how does it feel to be totally out of control? Come on tell us," laughed Sydney. "So, Ethan, told you everything? Well, girlfriend, you have been gone for four hours, so Ethan must have had a lot to say. Now this is the time that you got to spill all the beans, so tell us what happened."
Liz took a deep breath, "You guys will not believe it. I gave Ethan, ten minutes and I cannot tell you where the three hours and fifty minutes went. This morning has been a very overwhelming morning for me. First, guys, how could you? You all are supposed to be my dearest of friends. How could you?" Liz poured out her heart about the encounter she had this morning. Her eyes filled with amazement and joy as she told the story of her and Ethan. Her journey took her and her friends into the bliss and joy of a newfound love. As she tells of her unveilings, soft tears are shed by all, hands are held, and laughter filled the room. "Then to my surprise, Ethan, took me by my hands and pulled me directly in front of him. And said, Liz, I know you do not know me well. I really do not want to frighten you at all. But I really like you so much. My desire is not to just like you, but if you would give me the opportunity, I would like to fall in love with you."

All the ladies screamed "What! Liz, what did you say?"

"Well, you would be so proud of me, because I did not give in to the moment. I kept my composure and I was strong. I looked him right back in his eyes and softly said to Ethan, 'Ethan, you are correct. I do not know you. And yes, all of this is very frightening to me as well. But what you ask of me I cannot do.' "

Belinda, quickly interrupted and stood up and screamed, "Liz! What are you doing?"

"Belinda, it's all right. It is truly all right. I told Ethan he was granted that opportunity, but the rest of his condition has nothing to do with me." All the ladies laughed and gave each other high fives.

"Yes, that's it girl. You have learned well from the get-go, put the ball in his court. The Bible says, 'a man who finds a wife.' The work is on him! Just sit back and look good girl. Make him work from the beginning to the end. You have learned well from us. I guess you are ready," laughed Belinda.

"Now, Liz, here comes the important part. You have dinner with his family tonight, right?"

"Yes, and I am so nervous. Help me guys. Right now, my stomach is in a big knot."

"Well, ladies I am going to call Daniel to come and pick us up. It is shopping time. Liz, you have to find something so beautiful to wear to dinner tonight. Liz, you are meeting the family. Oh, my goodness. This is happening so fast," laughed Sydney.

All the ladies screamed, "Shopping! Yes, yes, yes!"

Chapter Seven

Converge

Clarence called Daniel trying to contact Sydney on the whereabouts of his kids. "Once again, man do not come calling me an asking me about your kids." yelled Daniel, "You should have been man enough and kept your word and got your kids, then you would know where they are. Do not call me again." Daniel hung up the phone quickly.

"Now, wait a minute. I know he does not think he is going to blow up my phone all night. Listen, man, I already told you to stop calling me and do not bother my sister. Do not go there man."

"Hey, guys let's go. Sorry ladies about ending our evening so soon. We need to go back to the beach house. This crazy cat, talkin' about coming to the beach house. I am not going to let him start stuff with my sister."

"Where is he at Daniel," asked Martinez.

"I am not sure Martinez, but let us cut him off before this freak gets into the gate."

"Yeah man, let us go."

Sydney called Daniel on the phone. "Daniel, Daniel, turn down your music. Where are you at?"

"I am heading to you. What's wrong," asked Daniel.

"Wrong? Who said anything was wrong? I need you to come and take us shopping."

"Uh, me and the ladies are hanging out now."

"Okay, Daniel, remember you are supposed to be our transportation this week.
"I am sorry, Sis. I thought you guys did not need me today. So, me and the fellas took the ladies out."
"Okay, I will uber it. Tell Myra and Samantha we are going shopping, and we will see them when they get back. Hey, Daniel, stay out of trouble.' '
"Hey, Sis, don't worry I got this."
"Yeah, that is exactly what I am concerned about. Bye, Daniel."
"Daniel, man why didn't you tell her about old boy coming?"
"Man, Martinez, this is her last day with the ladies. I do not want her upset about this craziness. We will hang out at the Beach Bar and we can see him if he comes.

Teddy called Robert. "Robert, how many times do you think I am going to call you man? One more time, Robert and I was about to stop calling you. What is wrong with you?"
"Man, Teddy you know, Amanda and Liz are both gone."
"Oh, yeah," laughed Teddy, "Boy, you are messed up. All your helpers are gone."
"Shut up man. I know. Did you get your wife on the phone? I do not know why they are not answering their phones?"
"No, I didn't get her, but I called Sydney's brother Daniel and he was there."
"Good did you tell him to tell my wife and my assistant to call me?"
"No, I told him to tell all the women to call their husbands."

"Okay, now you know I need Liz to call me too. I cannot find a certain brief."

"No, I did not. Yesterday at dinner you said you wanted Amanda to call you. You did not say Liz. Then you called Matt and asked him the same thing too? What is wrong with you man? You are completely lost without them."

"Shut up, I know what I asked you." Robert mumbled to himself, they left me with all these things to do. What in the world am I to do. I cannot find anything."

"Hey, Matt is on the phone. Matt did Robert say anything about contacting Liz?"

"Man, Teddy, why do you and Robert always call me and put me in the middle of your disagreements. I do not care. The only thing I care about is, did you get in contact with my wife? Why did all of them turn their phones off?"

"No, I told Robert I didn't get her, but I called Sydney's brother, Daniel, and he was there. And I told him to tell all the wives to call their husbands. But now Robert is mad because I did not tell Liz to call him directly."

"Yeah," laughed Matt, "Let me see, I do not know which one of them the brother is more lost without, Amanda or Liz?"

"Funny, make your jokes. But I will say it again. If any of your wives call you, please tell them to have Liz call me. It is important. Now, I have told you both."

Teddy's phone rang. "Wait one minute, guess what! My honey is calling me first. I got to go. And yes, Robert, I will tell her to tell Liz to call you."

"Hey, honey, how are you? And how are my boys," asked Sharon.

"Man, I miss you. You got to come home."
"Teddy, how are my boys?"
"Missing their mom. They are at my mom's house. She wanted them for a couple days. Come on babe, can't you just come home? The boys are gone and it's a perfect time for us to be together."
"I miss you too, babe. I will be home soon."
"Listen, Sharon, the boys are gone this weekend. So if you come home now, we will have plenty of time to be together just you and I."
"Honey, you are so sweet, but I will be home soon."
"Listen, Teddy, I am going to tell you a secret. You cannot say anything."
"Yeah you know me babe, I can keep a secret. What is it?"
"Amanda is pregnant with twins."
"What! You are kidding me? Twins? You mean Robert is going to be a dad?"
"Yep! Everyone except Myra is excited. You know her?"
"Ah, she does not count."
"Teddy, okay, my bag. I cannot wait. He talked all that stuff about no kids, and now he is having two at one time. He is going to be out of his mind. I love it. Robert is going to be a dad. Hey, what is she having?"
"We will not know until next week when she comes from the doctor."
"Great! Hey, I wonder if mom and dad knows?"
"Teddy do not say a word. Let her tell mom and dad."
"Okay, babe. How are you?"
"I'm having a good time."

"How are things going?"
"I am enjoying seeing everyone. Sydney's beach house is so beautiful. Rebecca has spoiled us with a chef, housekeeper, and massage therapist, so we can relax and catch up with each other.
"So you are getting plenty of rest, huh?" Even with the kids there?"
"Oh, no, Rebecca and Liz, surprised Sydney. Rebecca had Matthew fly them to Sydney's mom and dad's house in Kentucky."
"Hey, that's great."
"That means it's just you and the ladies. Hey, Daniel told me that Myra is there. I know she has clowned or something to make ya'll upset?"
"Well, she's been hanging out mostly with her friend Sam, and I know she was glad when she heard Sydney's kids were gone."
"Babe, who is Sam?"
"Sam is Samantha, and this is my first time meeting her too. She flew in with Liz and Rebecca, so I have not had a chance to really talk to her either."
"Well, when I talked to Daniel, he said he was interested in her, but he did not know if she was married or not."
"Oh, no, Sam is not married.
"Well, good. I told Daniel he needed to find out first."
"Well, if you talk to him again, you can tell him she is not married."
"Okay, babe. I just wanted to hear your voice. I really miss you. I hope you do not plan on doing this again, because the answer is no, in advance," laughed Teddy.

"It will be all right, Teddy. I love you and I promise I will call you before I go to bed. All of us promised to put away our phones, but we can call our honeys just before we go to bed."
"Babe, who made up that rule? Liz? "Hey, speaking of Liz, she went on a date last night."
"What, on a date? With whom?"
"The guy next door. He is a housekeeper. Wait honey, someone is calling me."
"Okay, I am coming," yelled Sharon."
"Okay, honey, I really have to go."
"Wait, no, Sharon, what do you mean she went on a date with the guy next door? Did you say he was the housekeeper?"
"Okay, I am coming," yelled Sharon.
"Ah, honey it's all good I will call you later and explain more. Love you, bye. "But he really is not. Wait, honey. I got to go, call you later, bye."
"Hey, no. Okay. She hung up." Teddy stopped and thought, "what in the world is going on there? I got to call the guys.

"Hey, man. Mark, this is Teddy have you heard from Belinda?"
"No, man. I tried calling her but no answer."
"Well, my boys are at my mom's, so a brother is as free as a bird. I am going to catch up with Robert and see if he want to hang."
"Teddy, now you know about pulling Robert away from work."
"Yeah, you are right, man."
"Well, he needs to get out. With Amanda gone, he needs to do something else besides work."

Robert called Matthew. "Hey Robert, man I missed Rebecca's call," said Matthew. "I was at practice. Did you hear from your wife, Amanda?"
"Yeah, she called. But it is no use, neither her nor Liz are coming back."
"Robert, man what are you talking about? Did you really expect them to?"
"Yeah, once I told them how everything is a mess."
"Hold on, wait, this is Teddy on the other line."
"Hey, Teddy, what's up?"
"Hey, I got Mark with me, how about you coming and hanging with your brothers Robert? The wives are all gone. We might as well make the best of it and have some fun."
"Hey, man. Wait. Hold on Teddy, I am talking to Matt on the other line. Let me conference you in."
"Hey, Teddy"
"Hey, Matt. Did you hear from your wife?"
"No, man. When she called, I was at practice and the shower. But guess what? A brother got the rest of the week off."
"Great man. What about you Robert, did you hear from Amanda?"
"Yeah, man."
"What's wrong with you?"
"Listen to this Teddy, he is upset because Amanda or Liz, will not come back and help him."
"Matt, listen, to this. Robert actually called his wife and asked her and Liz to come home," laughed Teddy. "Man you are so wrong. Man, you got to stop being so selfish."
"I am not selfish," yelled Robert.

"Robert, no, man, you cannot ask them to come home because you are having a hard time managing without them," said Matthew.

"I know. Robert you are my boy and all, but man you are too selfish. You want them to come back and help you. What about what they want?"

"I, know man, but, well," Robert respond with frustration.

"I know, go on and just admit it. You need someone. You know the more I think about this, I think God put you in this position, man. Bro, you got to open up. You are so afraid to let anyone know that you need them. Maybe you need Liz for work, but you are crazy missing Amanda. I know what is wrong. You did not expect to miss both of them so much," said Matthew.

"Matt, he is in so much pain because he misses his wife. Guess what, bro? I bet you have not ever felt this way. Yeah, yeah, I see they needed to leave your behind right here, so you can suffer. I can hear it now, 'Amanda, I cannot even breathe without you.' Now, say I am not right bro?"

"It does not matter, man. Teddy, she still will not come home even though she knows how much I miss her. She said she will be home soon."

"Robert, you know these ladies have been waiting all year for this week to be together. Hey, man, you know those ladies love sitting around talking about their kids, back in the day, shoes, shopping, and whoever knows what else."

"Yeah, and I heard from Sharon that Liz went on a date with this guy who is a housekeeper that works next door."

"What!" shouted Robert, "a housekeeper from next door. Man, Teddy, that sounds crazy."

"I know. I am not too happy with that either. But Sharon had to get off the phone and said she will tell me more later. But I hope that is not true. Cause, if things work out with them, man Robert, looks like you might lose Liz," Teddy and Matt broke out into laughter.

"Man, Teddy, stop. You are crazy. Liz, is not getting with no dude that is a housekeeper, so just quit it. You are just trying to get me worked up."

"Okay, man, I am just fooling with you, but you are selfish."

"Yeah, I know. This is the first time my wife has been gone this long away from me.

"Man, those ladies when they get together, they have so many stories. They will be talking for days. Sharon told me that Myra brought a new friend with her. Somebody by the name of Sam. Uh, yeah Samantha, or something like that!"

"What! What," yelled Matthew. "Did you say Samantha?"

"Man, no! Matt, tell me this not the Sam you told me about?"

"Tell me you are kidding me, Teddy?"

"Uh, I am not kidding man and what in the world is going on?"

"Okay, if this is so, I am on my way there right now!"

Teddy turned and looked at them, "Matt? Robert? Could somebody tell me what is going on?"

"Hold up, man. "Roy! Roy! Hey, Roy, called Alex and tell him to get my plane ready now!"

"Wait, hold up Matt, what are you going to do? Man, don't you think you need to talk to Rebecca first?"

"No, no, man I know Becky. She will just try her best to make the best of it. But I do not want that crazy woman around my wife ever. I do not want my wife to be on vacation tolerating her at all. So no, I am going there and getting her right now!"

"Man, Robert, you do not understand. Let me get off this phone. I already told you I know my wife. She's so sweet and she will try her hardest to not make waves. I do not want her there like that."

"Okay, Matt, I am going with you."

"Hey, I am also going, Robert. Hey, you guys are not leaving me."

"Hey, Mark, man something is up with Matt's wife and he is flying to the ladies, are you going?"

"What, well I guess, yeah."

"Hey, we are all going with you too, Matthew," said Teddy.

"I do not have a problem with it, just be ready at the airport at six o'clock your time. I will scoop you up. Listen, if you guys are not there, I am not going to wait."

"Okay, we understand man, just calm down. We'll see you at six o'clock."

"Robert, this airport is so crowded," said Teddy.

"Come on, Teddy, over here."

"Gentlemen, may I help you?"

"Yes, we are meeting Mr. Matthew Whitman."

"Your name and I.D., please. All right, have a seat over there. It's on time and will arrive in thirty minutes."

"Man, we got to find a way to calm this brother down. Did Robert at least call Rebecca, and tell her he was coming?"

"No."

"Well, the last time I talked to him he had not called her yet."

"I understand. I would be furious at Amanda too if she had kept any secrets from me too."
"I do not know, Robert, maybe she was handling it and did not want to upset Matt. Rebecca is a very smart lady."
"I know how he feels. No man wants his wife keeping secrets from him. Rebecca should have told Matt right away about that girl. Man, now I do not know what is running through his mind. And just think man, that crazy girl has been there for four days."
"Man, Robert, this do not sound like Rebecca. She is just like my Belinda, very careful about everything. Maybe there is some kind of mix up."
"Yeah, I agree with Mark. Robert, do not get me wrong, I do not blame him for being mad. But maybe she has a good reason."
"Good reason? Listen to yourself, Teddy. For me and Amanda, I told her we have no secrets. Our number one rule, no secrets. We must tell each other first. No secrets."
"No, man, you need to listen to yourself. Our number one rule?"
"Man, Mark did you hear that?"
"What kind of talk is that when it comes to your wife? I think you have been in the law game so long that you have checked out of real life. You need to get a grip, Robert, 'our number one rule.' Man, this is your wife you have to trust her."
Mark looked at the both of them, shook his head and said, "Hey, man, why don't you all table this before it gets out of hand."

"No, Mark! Teddy is the one that needs to get a grip," yelled Robert.

"No. Come on guys do not start this. Not here and not now."

"No, man! Mark, Teddy, I think you hold that attitude because you played around so much in the past and kept up so many lies and secrets that it's okay for someone, especially your wife not to be honest, because you used to be so dishonest."

"What? Robert, man what in the world are you talking about? How can you bring up what I use to do?"

"Well, here it goes guys. I warned you." Mark walked away and shook his head.

"Teddy needs to watch what he is saying to me, Mark, talking about I need to check into reality. What's that about?"

"No, that is not it. Yeah, I had a past, but I am a changed man. And you are wrong, it is not because I use to be a player and lie. It is because I simply trust my wife. I trust that if Sharon is not telling me something, it is for a good reason. I do not need to make up rules to rule my wife. Perhaps you should start trusting your wife instead of setting up rules."

"Boy, Teddy, listen. You do not know anything about my relationship with Amanda, and whether I trust her or not, nothing. So I suggest you step away and mind your own business and leave me alone. Because the way I see it, you've got one wife, two children from two baby mamas, so don't you think you got enough business than to be talking to me about mine."

"Well, I got one more thing and it's your business. I know that you are having twins. Now, how you like me now?"

Robert stands up.

"Gentlemen, your flight has arrived, we are ready for you to board. This way please."

Mark, Robert, and Teddy swiftly walked down the corridor. Robert looked back at Teddy, "Teddy, what in the world are you talking about? Who told you that? How do you know that?"

"Oh, well, Robert, I guess I do know something about your business, right? I guess so much for trying to set rules for your wife, right? Funny, huh? Sharon is the only wife that has called, and I know your secret. All without a rule."

Robert walked lifelessly to his seat and dropped down.

"Hey, man, what's wrong with you," Matthew turned and looked at Teddy. "Hey man, I mean, what is up with Robert?"

"Man, ask him? Since he wants to bring up a brother's past and all."

"Mark, what is going on with them?"

"Matt, the same old stuff. Both of them always go too far."

"Come on, Robert you didn't do that again, did you? Man, we all talked about that at the last Man-2-Man meeting with P.C. at church. I thought you guys put that away."

"I have apparently," said Teddy, "but obviously, Robert has not. I know I used to be messed up, but I also know it is apparent that I am a changed man. When we were at Man-2-Man, P.C. asked all of us to just forgive and rebuild our brotherhood with each other. I know I did some things that hurt Robert in the past, but it's been how many years? I am married and I have a great wife, which I have never even thought about cheating on. I have two great boys who I swore never to hurt. I have a family which I am proud to say I love and give my life for. It is painful to keep being reminded of my past." As Teddy's eyes become glassed over, he continued, "One day, I had some struggles, I am not going to lie to you. Something happened and I became bored, or not satisfied, I do not know. Hey, me and my wife we talked. Man, I am so grateful for her. She was not upset or threatened. She said let us go and talked to P.C. We met with them and P.C. talked with us. And he asked me, Teddy, I want you to ponder this question. 'When did Christ become not enough?' Man, I broke. I broke on the spot. Because I did not realize that was what I was saying. I had started neglecting getting in my Word, praying with my wife, and I missed several of the Man-2-Man monthly fasts. Man, I had begun to slip. Pastor prayed with us. I made a commitment to God and Sharon I would be faithful to the both of them. And guess what man? I have. And it is not even a struggle to do so. So, now man, Robert, I was wrong for telling you that Amanda is having twins. Sharon asked me to keep it a secret until Amanda told you, so I am sorry for that."

"What! This is great news, Robert!" said Matt. "Mark, Mark did you hear this man Robert is going to be a father?" shouted Matt again.

"Yeah! Teddy told me this morning. I think it's great."

Matthew turned to Robert, "Man, are you kidding me? You are upset because she did not tell you first? How on earth does that overshadow the magnitude of the news?"

"Well, I was not the first to know," Robert said sadly.

"Robert, all of us know that those ladies always tell each other first. Wow, Robert, and twins, too! Wow, man this is so great!"

"Teddy, you are right man. I am sorry, forgive me, bro. There is no excuse for what I said to you. I was just wrong, dead wrong. I am sorry for hurting you. I have watched you and I really wish I could be more like you man. I know I have never told you that, but I have watched you with your kids and you are a great dad. I just think I would just mess kids up. Now, look at me. My wife didn't even trust me to tell me first."

"No, no, man. Robert, do not take it like that. Man, I am telling you that those ladies always talk to each other. None of us will know first, but it is cool. That's just the way they do things man."

"Man, thanks Matthew but Teddy is right. I think I am so afraid of being hurt that I may have put too much pressure on Amanda. When I say Amanda does everything for me, she does. I know she loves me so much. And for the first time, I see how selfish I have been. She has been asking me for over a year to talk about having children. All I thought about was the impact it would have on my life. All the while thinking that I am talking about our life. Yeah, Matthew I know our wives talk, but I believe I have made Amanda a little uncomfortable to tell me. I tell you that just messes me up. Something she wanted so badly, something so joyful for her, and she is unable to share that with me because she knows I might not feel the same way, or my reactions might hurt her. Man, right now I need P.C. Matthew, can I go in the back and call him."

"No need to ask, go on we will pray when you finish talking to P. C."

"Hey, Matt, man how are you holding up," asked Teddy.

"Man, Teddy, I called P.C. before I took off. And he prayed with me and talked with me, so I am doing better. At least the intense anger is gone. P.C. told me that I have to trust Rebecca. He knows that I love her and want to protect her, but I got to trust that she knows what to do. But I told him that I am still going to check on my wife," laughed Matt.

"What did P.C. say?"

"Hey man, you know P.C., He said, he would do the same if it was his El."

"Yeah, you know that's the truth," laughed Teddy.

As the afternoon ticked away, all are unaware that their lives will converge. While the ladies are out shopping and so excited about Liz having dinner with Ethan's family and her prospect of new love, they laughed and remembered the good old days. Remembering just how skinny they all were. Like high school girls, they are enjoying their shopping trip.

They are unaware that Clarence is on his way to contend with Sydney over the whereabouts of his children. Daniel, his friends, Myra, and Samantha, are waiting at the Beach Bar for Clarence. Ethan and his family are preparing dinner and to meet Liz. Matthew's plane just landed and is filled with anxious husbands. Matthew anxiously wants to see Rebecca, due to Samantha being there. Robert is upset about not being told first from Amanda that they are having twins, both him and Teddy are concerned about Liz having a mystery-housekeeper date. With less than an hour, the convergence will happen. All the lives at Mission Impossible will be forever changed.

Chapter Eight
The Answer is Yes

"Hello, Ethan," Rebecca, frantically waved her hands to silence all the ladies. Whispering, "Hey guys, quiet. It is Ethan." They all stood quietly awaiting to hear. "Liz, what did he want," asked Belinda.

"To tell me he will be here to pick me up at six thirty p.m."

"Okay, ladies, we have to get moving. It simply not enough time. We have less than three hours to turn Liz, from beast to beauty," laughed Belinda.

"Not so," laughed Liz, "you mean from beauty to beautiful."

"Hey, Daniel, it's Teddy."

"Hey, Teddy, what's up?"

"What is the address to the beach house?"

"Man, what's up? You coming here or something? Is something wrong?"

"Yeah, man. We are already here, so what is the address?

"Okay, thanks Daniel."

"Wait, hold on Teddy. You got a minute? I got to tell you something. I am here with my boys waiting at the beach house looking out for Sydney's crazy ex, because he is threatening to come to the beach house and confront her about the whereabouts of his kids."

"Hey, man, how long ago did this all happen?"

"A couple of hours ago."

"Are the ladies at the house?"
"No, Liz, and a couple of them are out shopping and two of the ladies are with me."
"Uh, is one of them that girl you talked to me about?"
Teddy laughed, "Yeah, man, you remembered."
"Yeah. Well, okay, we are on our way. We will catch up with you when we get there."
"Hey, man, you will see me. I am in an ivory Escalade."
"We are in a black Lincoln. See you in a few."
"Teddy, what is going on," asked Robert.
"Daniel, Sydney's brother, said that her ex-husband is upset because she will not tell him where his kids are at. This cat, Clarence, is headed to her beach house to confront her about the whereabouts of his kids."
Matthew shook his head, "Man, this man is crazy. First, he refused to take the kids and now he wants them. Becky, when she first got there, called me, and told me what this cat did. She asked me if I would fly them out to Kentucky to be with their grandparents for the week."
"Who has custody of the kids," asked Robert.
"Becky told me that Sydney does."
"Well, that guy can forget it. She has the right to fly them to the moon if she wishes. He might as well not waste his time going there. I tell you what is going to happen is, this cat is either going to jail, if she calls the police or get a beat down or both," laughed Robert.
Matthew shook his head, "What a shame. What man does not have custody or even joint custody of his kids? I mean, that's crazy."

"Man, Matthew, I see this all the time in the courts. Men who are not taking care of their children, and then put all kinds of demands and pressure on their kid's moms. They have to be dragged to court to pay their child support and many of them spend no time with their own kids. It is just foolishness. How is the next generation supposed to have a fighting chance at success. If their fathers do not even care enough to have joint custody of them? Man, it's just sad."

"Precisely why I got my two sons, Robert. I know I made my mistakes early on, but I realized if I want different for them it starts with me. I thank God that I am a changed man," said Teddy.

"Yeah Teddy, I am proud of you, Teddy. You took care of your kids before you gave your heart to Christ," said Robert.

"Right, Matt, but I am a better father now. Now, I am a man of God. Now, God tells me how to raise my boys. Remember when Pastor told us that despite the fact that we may have grown up without our fathers, Christ requires us to make sure we are there for our kids. He said that our Heavenly Father is our perfect example of Fatherhood. Robert, we are blessed to have our dad, who is a real man of God around us. When we grew up, we did our own thing. Well, you see how well that worked out. Both of us are right back with the Lord."

"Man, I wish. You know my father was absent from my life. I love my mom, and she did a great job. But it was painful not to have a dad at my games and help me with stuff. Thank God for my granddad who acted like my dad. I would be lost without Pops. He came to all my games, and he was there when I signed my contract. Man, my kids love him. They think that he is their grandpa and not their great-granddad. But I always told myself, when I became a dad, no matter what, I would never leave my children," said Teddy.

"Man, I am with you. Another thing, Matt, I was determined that no other man will raise my children but me. My dad raised me, and I am raising my sons."

"Yeah, Teddy, and you know our dad and mom were not hearing that about us not taking care of our kids. I do not have respect for a man who does not take care of his children," said Robert.

"Man, me either. I feel sorry for Sydney. I hope I get a chance to talk to this guy," said Mark.

"Well, Mark, better you than me. I do not have any respect for him. Every day, I see too many guys like him filling up the court rooms." said Robert.

As the ladies shopped in preparation for Liz's dinner with Ethan's, parents," Rebecca yelled excitedly, "Hey, ladies I got it, so let us go now. They can take her in twenty minutes. Let's go."

Liz looked around. "Wait, I did not agree to getting my hair done.

It looks just fine to me. What is wrong with my hair," asked Liz as she looked at them.

"I love my sister but trust us on this one," laughed Belinda.

Sydney, pulling Liz, "Enough girl, now come on."

"Listen, guys, I am grateful that you guys are so excited. But I do not want you to make too much out of this yet. We are just getting to know each other. We are not an official couple or anything. I am having dinner with his family. That is all."

"So that's what you have been telling yourself, "laughed Rebecca, as she looked around at Belinda and Sydney.

"Liz, look at me. You are right. We are very excited, but you are wrong about everything else. This is not any old dinner. No man sets up for you to meet his parents unless he is serious about you. What is it, Liz? Are you afraid of falling in love with him?"

Liz looked a little dazed. "I guess, Rebecca. I guess I am still shocked that everything has happened so fast. I mean I have been here a week today. A guy has asked to date me exclusively, and I am meeting his parents. It is like a whirlwind. I mean what is next? The problem with this is why am I not apprehensive about the whole thing. Let's face it. Things do not really happen this fast, right?"

Belinda looked at Liz, "Girl, I do not call six years fast. At least that is how long I have been praying for you. Ever since your breakup with Tony, I have been praying for you to meet the right man who would love you for you. I truly hope this is the guy. I have asked God to bless your life with a good spouse. Liz, I am really proud of you. I know the last relationship was crazy and very painful for you. But I have watched you firsthand, and how much you have grown in God. He has become your enough. You have allowed Christ to build your life. Even when Tony came back to you and asked to start the relationship over, I was for sure you would. I knew when you did not, that Christ had become your enough. That is when I knew you had truly moved on and wanted to build a life in Him.

I love you for trusting God during a very painful time in your life. I truly hope he is the one, because I would love to be with you and help you plan this wedding," said Rebecca.

"Amen to that," said Belinda.

"Liz, she has not done all the praying. I too prayed and fasted for you during these six years as well. I was so hurt by what you went through, but I knew just like the Lord healed my broken heart, He would heal yours if you trusted Him. The Scripture I would pray one about how Jesus came to heal the broken hearted. I, too, hope Ethan is the one. Because nothing would give me more pleasure than to help plan your wedding," said Rebecca.

"Wow, I love you guys! But let's not talk about the wedding just yet. Let me just focus on dinner first. Any more is a bit overwhelming. I must confess, I am a little frightened by the possibility. But right now, ladies, I am just going to take it one step at a time. Right now, first things first. Tonight I am having dinner with a very special guy, who I really like, and I am looking forward to really getting to know him. How about that for starters?"

"Perfect Liz. And on that note, we are here. So, let's go get gorgeous, girl."

The guys plane landed and they called to meet up with Daniel.

"Hey man, Daniel, right?"

"Yeah, man, this is Teddy."

"Teddy, has Sydney's ex-husband arrived at the beach house?

"Not yet. I will take you guys to the house and open the door for you."

"Thanks, I appreciate that man." All the guys drove to the beach house.

"Hey, nice house, man," said Teddy.

"Thanks. Make yourselves comfortable. The ladies should be back in a few. They all have gone shopping because Liz is going to dinner with old boy next door. Hey, man, let me know if I can do anything for you?"

"Wait, man uh, Daniel, right?"

"Yeah man."

"I'm Robert. Liz, is my cousin and I am her boss, too. Do you know anything about this man that Liz is seeing? Is he a housekeeper or what?"

Suddenly, the all the guys turned to see who is knocking so hard and yelling at the door. "Open the door, Daniel! Open the door or I will break it down! I know you are in there. Where is Sydney? Where are my kids?" All the guys raced to the door.

"Man, what in the world wrong with you! First, back up off the door," yelled Daniel.

"What is going on here, Daniel? Who are all these men? Where is Sydney and where are my kids? You are such a liar! You said Sydney was here with her girlfriends. Liar! Then who are all these guys? Which one is seeing my wife? Which one of you think you are going to play daddy with my kids? Wait, I know you. You are Matthew Whitman. Man how you doing? Are you with my wife?" Immediately, Roy jumped up and walked and in between Clarence and Matthew.

Daniel turned to Clarence and said, "Clarence you need to shut up. You are making a fool out of yourself."

"It's Okay, Roy. Your name is Clarence, right?"

"Yes." said Clarence.

"Yes and my name is Matthew. And no, I am not seeing your wife or playing daddy with your kids. I have my own wife and kids. As a matter of fact, there is not one man here seeing your wife or playing daddy with your kids. Clarence a bit of advice right now. Look around you. I believe this is a good time and in your best interest to just go outside, calm down, and listen."

Clarence looked at everyone and turned to go outside, but he sees Sydney's car pull up and he walked swiftly to the door.

Sydney, looked out the window. "What in the world is going on? Who are all these people? Why is Clarence here? Why are your husband's here? What has happened? Why are all of them here?" Rebecca, frantically looked around, "Oh, my goodness Liz, where is Samantha? Where is Matt?" As the driver brought the car to a rolling stop, all the ladies leaped out to meet the guys who all ran out of the house. Clarence ran up to Sydney. Suddenly, a body stepped in between him and Sydney.

"Excuse, me, sir. I believe you were asked to leave and cool off, right," said Roy.

Sydney, looked confused as Clarence quickly stepped back from her.

"Thank you, sir," said Roy.

Sydney looked around at everyone in total disbelief. "Listen, I do not know what in the world is going on and why everyone is here. Everyone needs to calm down, and go into the house, and let us sit down, so we can find out why all of you guys are here." As everyone walked to the house, Sydney turned to Daniel, "Daniel where is Myra and Samantha?"

"Oh, I left them at the Beach Bar."

"Please go and get them, Daniel. Thank you. Everyone please come on in and take a seat." Looking curiously at them, Sydney welcomes everyone. "First, welcome all of you. Now, could you please explain to us why all of you guys are here?"

Softly, Matthew turned to Rebecca, and asked, "Becky, babe why didn't you tell me that Samantha was here? Babe, I talked to you several times, and you said nothing about her being here. Please tell me why did all you ladies stop answering your phones? I was not sure if you were all right."

"Wait, one minute. I do not mean to intrude, but Matthew, do not tell me that it was Daniel who told you that Samantha was here, right," asks Sydney.

"Well, no. I found out when I talked to Teddy."

"But it does not matter. Becky, you should have told me."

"Whoa, wait, hold up I can explain," said Teddy looking at Sharon.

"Yes, do explain Teddy. I really want to hear this," said Sharon.

"Well, babe. Mark and I were hanging out at the house, and I was talking to Robert and Matt on the phone. We were all trying to help out Robert when I told him about all of you. Then suddenly Matt became very upset once he heard that old girl, uh, whatever her name was here."

Sharon quickly interrupted Teddy, "Her name is Samantha, Teddy, Samantha."

"Yes, you are right Sharon that's her name. However, things really got out of control after Robert found out about Amanda, and Liz seeing a housekeeper. Matthew said we had to leave right now to come and see about Rebecca. So I called Daniel and he told us about the situation with Clarence coming here to threaten Sydney about their kids. It was then that Daniel told me about old girl." Teddy looked at Sharon, "I mean he told me that Samantha was here with the other ladies."

"Yes, Sydney. Where are my kids," yelled Clarence.

Sydney immediately turned to Clarence, "Clarence, please, be quiet. I will tell you where your kids are in a few."

"Okay, let me guess. Robert you got your news from Teddy, too," asked Belinda.

Robert stared at Amanda and softly answered, "Yes."

"Teddy, let me guess. Sharon told you, but I know you my dear brother, she swore you to secrecy, right," asked Belinda

"Teddy, answered with his head down, "I am sorry, honey."

"Now, Teddy, did Daniel tell you that Liz has a date with the housekeeper next door, too?" asked Sydney

Teddy slowly answered, "Yes, he did."

Sydney looked about, smiled and, said, "Well, it appears that everyone here has some explaining to do. All of you guys are welcome to use any part of the house." As Sydney counted all of her guests, she called Chef Rio. "We will have guests for dinner. Please prepare for about ten attendees."

Clarence heard Sydney's request to Chef Rio, smiled looked around and counted. "Hey, Sydney, you missed two guests."

"No, Clarence, I didn't. You will not be staying for dinner. So please go right now out to the deck, or I will have you escorted off the property, and you still will not know where your kids are." So please, Clarence, meet me on the deck."

"Wow, Sydney, why so hard? What have I ever done to you?"

Sydney ignored Clarence's comment as she talked to Chef Rio. "What time should we expect dinner please?"

"Seven p.m., sharp."

"Thank you."

Each couple found their private places and unwrapped their stories. Peace began to fill the air. "Mark, are you all right," asked Belinda.

"Yes, sweetheart I am. I came along so I can have an excuse to see and be with you," said Mark.

"Good, if you don't mind, I am going to help Liz get ready to go to dinner."

"Wait, Belinda. What is going on with Liz? Is she seeing a housekeeper?"

"Mark, well, yes and no."

"Huh?"

"Come over here baby and let me show you something. Do you see that house over there?"

"Wow, Belinda this beach is incredible. No wonder you guys did not call us and hung out at the beach all day. Whoa, look at this. Is that where he works?"

"Yes, he is the keeper of that house, and he is also the owner of that house."

"What? Are you kidding me! The guy Liz is having dinner with tonight owns that house? That house? That house is owned by that guy?"

"Mark, honey, no matter how many ways you ask, the answer is yes. But baby, it is a long story. I will tell you after I help Liz, get ready. Ethan, will be here at sixty-thirty. Oh, my we have less than an hour to get ready."

"Yes, you help her get ready, Belinda. Yes, you do that, sweetheart. Hey, I am going to go down to the beach. Come down and join me when you finish."
"Okay, love you." said Belinda.
"Love you too. Now go on and help Liz. She needs to make a good impression."

"Hey, man," said Ethan
"Hey, how are you," asked Mark.
"I am fine, and you," asked Ethan.
"Awesome beach," said Mark
"Yeah, it's nice," said Ethan.
"Hey, man I do not mean to pry. Are you all right? I mean you keep pacing back and forth and staring at my friend's house?"
"Is Liz our friend," asked Ethan.
"Wait, how do you know Liz," asked Mark.
"Do you know Liz too," asked Ethan.
"Wait, I asked you first. How do you know my cousin," asked Mark.
"Liz is your cousin? Oh, oh, man, I am sorry. I do not mean to be rude. It is just that I am so nervous. I am Ethan from next door." "Oh, you are the guy Liz is having dinner with this evening. You are the undercover-housekeeper guy," laughed Mark.
Ethan stopped and broke out in laughter. "So, you heard about that?"
"Yes man. My name is Mark and I am married to Liz's, cousin, Belinda."

"Yes, I have had the pleasure of meeting your wife at the Bible studies we had on the beach. She is a wonderful woman."

"Yes, she is, so why are you so nervous," asked Mark.

"Liz is so important to me. I want to connect with her before she leaves. I have made a bold step by having my family at dinner tonight. Well, once my mom found out I had a tiny spark of interest, she jumped at the chance to come and meet her. Well, of course my father followed her. I am hoping that Liz does not become overwhelmed, and I think I am moving too fast. You know Mark, right? Please tell me what you think," asked Ethan.

"Well, you have a point. I do know her and yes, she will become overwhelmed if she thinks things are going too fast. Hey, man just make dinner just about dinner. Do not talk about relationship, just have dinner. Keep the conversation away from relationship. She will be fine. Just relax and have fun tonight. Nothing serious and you will be okay."

"Thanks so much. Yes, I really appreciate you talking to me. I have to pick her up in about twenty minutes. I better get ready. Thanks again, you really helped me. It's good to meet you. She didn't tell me her family was coming in."

"No, it was a surprise. I tell you what, when you come to pick her up, I will introduce you to her other two cousins. They are here, too."

"Great! I look forward to meeting them also. See you at six-thirty, Mark," said Ethan.

"Sure, thing, Ethan," said Mark.

Amanda moved slowly to the window in her bedroom, and stared outside watching the sunset on the beautiful beach water, waiting in anticipation for Robert's disapproval. Robert came closely behind her, placed his head on her shoulder and whispered, "Honey, I am so very sorry." Amanda slowly turned and looked at him. As Robert pulled her close, he kissed her. "Amanda I am so sorry. Honey, I am not mad at you for not telling me first. I am sad, not because of the pregnancy either. I am sad because I have made you feel so uncomfortable to talk to me about it. I am sorry about that. I have been selfish. I am sorry for that. I love you with all my heart. The day you came into my life my whole world change. I could not believe I had such a treasure as you. I know, I am without excuse these past three or four years spending so much time at the firm. My problem is I am always worried about the business and I have forgotten about what is really important, that is us. Sorry for my strict stance on not having children. I am wrong. I know you stated repeatedly that you did not want to have children after forty. Well, I just, well, it has just saddened me to know you are carrying our children, which something you wanted so badly and that is so awesome and so special to you, but you could not share it with me or celebrate with me. It is not right, babe. And again, I am sorry. Please forgive me, Amanda." Amanda quickly pulled Robert and kissed him and whispered, "All is forgiven, honey. When I married you, I understood how important your business is to you. But we also talked about having a family, too. The wonderful thing is Robert, I was just as surprised as everyone else when I found out I was pregnant. Remember I had that awful cold? I took some antibiotics and

well, about a month later, we got pregnant. But to my utter amazement, when they told me twins, I could not believe it. I wanted to tell you, but I wanted to find the right timing. But believe me, honey, I planned on telling you after I came back from this trip." Amanda, again, softly kissed Robert. "Robert, honey, listen to me. You will make a great dad." Robert hugged Amanda tightly. "Honey thanks for believing in me. Thank you so much. I needed to hear that from you. Please tell me, Amanda all about our babies."
"Gladly, dear," laughed Amanda.

Mark meets Clarence on the beach.
"Hey, man. Clarence is my name, what's yours?"
"Mark, man."
"Let me ask you something. Do you have kids," asked Clarence.
"Yeah, I have two boys," said Mark.
"Both with the same moms," asked Clarence.
"Huh, what? Oh, yeah. Belinda is my wife. She is in there and we have two boys together."
"Okay, why do you ask," asked Mark.
"Man, my ex-wife is Sydney. She told me that I have to leave. She does not want me here. I just cannot seem to get it together. No matter how hard I try. Man, you know women. No matter what you do, nothing seems to be enough for them. You cannot please them. You know what I mean man," said Clarence.
"No, man. I absolutely do not know what you mean. That is not my philosophy when it comes to my wife."

"Huh, what? You said you are married right? Man, and you said your wife is satisfied? Get out of here. You are lying, right?"

Mark moved and stood directly in front of Clarence. "Let us start off right, Clarence. We do not really know each other. So, let us keep our conversation on that level. For starters, I am not a liar. I do not think that way about my wife at all. That kind of thinking leads to divorce."

"Okay, man. Hey, my bag. I was out of place. I do not believe you are a liar. But I have not heard a cat tell me that a woman can be satisfied. Satisfied with what we do? Come on man, be real. You see, I was once married, too. Well, let me say, things just did not work out. Hey, no matter what I did Sydney, was never satisfied, always arguing, and fighting. Man, I got tired of that. No matter what I did, she would find something that I did not do right. Man, nothing was ever good enough. So perhaps you have that one rare woman, that one in a million woman that can be satisfied. But all the cats I know, they are all singing the same song about their girlfriends and baby mamas. But man, what choice do we have? A man has to have a woman," laughed Clarence. "Man and we surely cannot live with them and you most surely cannot live without them. So, what do you do?"

"Well, I will have to agree with you on all points, except one. Yes, I have that rare woman and I love her dearly. Yes, I agree, all the cats you know may all be singing the same song, but no, you do have a choice. Your choice is to do what the Bible said to do. God tells a man, not some cats, to find a wife and not a woman."

"Well, I do not believe that God stuff, man. I don't go to church. Well, I went when I was little, and Sydney tried to get me to go to church with her when we were married, but I told her I'm not trying to hear that. Besides man, God is not real. Even if he was real, he isn't caring about what's happening here or with us."

"Listen, man. I know most men are too prideful to admit that in order for you or any man to attract this rare and one-in-a-million woman I told you about, you or they would need to be that rare and one-in-a-million man. Why should a woman settle for less than her own worth? If she is a woman than I think she deserves a man, not some fool. By the way, guess what Clarence? The Bible tells us the difference between a man and a fool."

"What? Who is a man and who is a fool?"

"Yeah, you said you do not believe in that God stuff. Well, the Bible says, the fool has said in his heart that there is no God. So Clarence, that could be one reason you cannot attract the rare woman that can be satisfied, because she requires a man and not a fool."

Clarence stepped back, and frowned as he looked at Mark. "Man, uh, what did you say your name is?

"Mark."

"Uh, Mark, you do not know me that well."

"I know you well enough to know that thing you do not believe in is the very thing you need. Let's be real. Why are you here? Not for your kids. You know that your ex is a good mother, and her kids are her heart. So why are you here, man? I know why you are here. Because you had a good wife, fooled around, emphasis on fooled around, got caught, and ended up divorced. And now you are the one not satisfied because you want your family back, and the thought of any man having your family is driving you nuts. You want your wife back because you want what you so foolishly gave up. Now, am I right?"

Clarence dropped down into the sand with his hands on his head and his eyes glassed over, "But man, I never thought I would lose my family. I am going nuts. I love my children and I love Sydney. It is so messed up I cannot think, sleep, or eat. Man, I cannot do anything. She is so stubborn and hateful. She does not understand. I told her, man, that girl had meant nothing to me, not compared to what we had. But she would not listen and she left, took my kids and crashed my life."

"No, Clarence, she did not do that. She only responded to your foolish acts. Your foolish acts of cheating and not taking care of your family caused you to lose your family. You want help, man? The first step is ownership to what you did. Again, you need God. Let me tell you. I do not care what woman you get, you will be back in the same position. You see, you are allowing lust to dominate your life. The Bible says lust is never satisfied, but love satisfies all. Right now, Clarence, the life you are living is not enough to satisfy you, right? After a while and after so many women but not real connections, high times turn into low times, and the club scene gets dull. Then you find yourself having to do things you never imagined doing."

"Yes, you are right man. I never meant well, it's too late." Clarence looked sorrowfully out at the ocean. "Man, I do not know. It's funny, Sydney just told me the same thing. Just before she told me to get out. She said this weekend she rededicated herself to God. She said that Liz prayed with her and God gave her great peace, and now she has a new relationship with God. For the first time she spoke to me softly and said she did not want to fight with me. She asked me if I would be willing to work on just being good parents to our kids. Man, that made me so mad. I cursed her and stormed away. But you know what man, uh, normally Sydney would have cursed me back, but she just stood there. And after I finished, without raising her voice, she calmly asked me to leave, and said she is praying for me. Man, what a monster am I? Why did I do that? Talking about doing things you never thought you would do. I love her but I know I am the last person on the planet she wants. And I know for the first time she was kind to me and I acted," Clarence looked at Mark, "I hate to say it, but a fool."

"Man, you need to give your life to God. He is your enough. He is the only one that can rescue you off the world's crazy roller coaster. God is the only one that can satisfy that lust craving. God is love. So, when you open your heart to Him, He will replace your lust with His love, hopelessness with His hope, unrest with rest. Man, Clarence I cannot promise if you come to God that he will put you and Sydney back together. But I can guarantee He can fix you, the man. If you would like, man, I can help you find his peace."

"Yes, man I need his peace, because I fear that Sydney is gone forever, and I do not know at this point how to handle that. So yeah, I need help, man."

"Okay, let's pray and you can ask Jesus into your heart, and ask him to make you into the man He wants you to be. Ask Him to make you into a son of God."

Daniel arrived at the Beach Bar to pick up Samantha and Myra. "Okay, ladies sorry about the delay. Had trouble at the house but all is good. The ladies husband's showed up so let's go back to the house," said Daniel.
"Uh, Daniel, did you say all the husbands are at the house now? Do you mean Matthew Whitman, too," asked Samantha.
"Yeah, that's the awesome thing. Matthew Whitman is at my sister's beach house in the flesh, baby. Wait. How do you know Matthew?"
"Myra, I do not believe it," said Samantha.
"Oh, my goodness Samantha, what are you going to do," asked Myra.
"What do you mean what is Samantha going to do? What do you have to do with Matthew," asked Daniel.

Meanwhile back at Mission Impossible. Liz heard the doorbell ring. "Okay, Liz, Ethan is here," shouted Belinda. "He is here, everyone come."
"Please tell me, Belinda. I must know the look on Robert's face."
"Girl like a deer in the headlights, deer in in headlights," laughed Belinda.
"Hey, Ethan, man what are you doing here?" asked Matthew
Ethan looked confused, "Matthew what are you doing here? Are you one of Liz's cousins?"

"No, no man. Well, they are like family, just good friends since college days. My wife is here, Rebecca. Wait do not tell me you are the housekeeper guy from next door?"
"In the flesh," laughed Ethan.
"So that was what Mark was talking about. Let me introduce you to her cousins. Hey, guys, come over here. Here is the mystery man himself, the housekeeper from next door. My friend and attorney, Mr. Ethan Grayson III. Liz's, date for tonight. This is Teddy her cousin and his brother, Robert. Who is not only her cousin but her boss, too."
"Hey, man, so you are not a housekeeper," asked Teddy.
"Well, no. Nice to meet you, Teddy." Teddy looked back at Robert. "Man, Robert, what is wrong with you man?"
"Huh?" Good afternoon Mr. Grayson."
"Huh? Good afternoon Mr. Grayson?" Teddy looked at Robert. "What is up with Robert," asked Teddy
"I am sorry Mr. Grayson. It is my pleasure to meet you."
"Robert, please call me Ethan."
Teddy looked around, "Wait. Wait. What am I missing? Why are you calling him Mr. Grayson? What is going on? Why is everyone acting so strangely? Okay, who are you? Some kind of movie star or something? Tell me what I have missed."
"Teddy, come here," said Sharon, "Honey, you are making Liz's date feel uncomfortable. Please, come here."
"I am uncomfortable, too, "Teddy walked to Sharon and he whispered, "What is going on?"
"I will tell you later."
"Hey everyone Liz is on her way out." Teddy I will tell you later," laughed Sharon.

Robert raced over to Liz's side. "Hey cousin you look just beautiful."
Everyone looked at Robert in shock.
"Ah, come on," yelled Teddy. "Okay, will someone tell me what is up with Robert?"
"Well, thank you cousin. I believe this is my first compliment from you ever," laughed Liz.
The room lit up with laughter.
"Hello, Liz. Are you ready," asked Ethan.
"Yes, I am Ethan."
"It was a pleasure meeting all of you. I promise I will not have her out too late."
"No, no, keep her. Have a good time, just keep her. You are just next door. Have a good time," Robert joyfully said.
"Honey, settle down," laughed Amanda.
"Ethan, we will wait up so be expecting us."
"Somehow I knew that, Rebecca."
"Good evening, everyone," said Ethan.
Teddy stood up. "Okay, I have held my peace long enough. Who is he and what is going on? And man, Robert what is with you? Mr. Grayson and stuff?"
"Wait, Robert allow me. Teddy, Mr. Ethan Grayson is the firm that handles all of my legal affairs and many Fortune 500 companies, actors, players, and so on. Grayson & Grayson are the creme de la creme of the legal world."
Teddy laughed and said, "Oh, Robert, boy you are in trouble now."
"Teddy, what are you talking about? I am in trouble now?"

"Because if this man is serious about Liz, and he asks her to marry him, she is gone."

Robert looked frantically at Amanda. "Teddy, Teddy be quiet. Just be quiet," yelled Robert. "It is a date, nothing more. Nobody is talking about marriage or losing anybody. It is just a date."

"Well, you keep on telling yourself that. It is a date and Liz, is meeting Ethan's parents tonight. Yeah, just keep telling yourself that until you get an invitation in the mail telling you to save the date," laughed Teddy.

Robert worriedly said, "You guys do not think that Liz would leave me? Do you all?"

"Man, Robert, you said it yourself. Do not pay attention to Teddy. It is just a date. Hey, wait you guys. You smell that? It is time for dinner and I am hungry. Let's go eat everyone." Robert walked past Teddy and smacked him on the head.

"You guys go on. I am going down to the beach and to get Mark," yelled Belinda.

Daniel arrived with the other ladies. "Hey, I am back. Where is everyone," yelled Daniel.

"Hey, everyone is at dinner. Where is Myra and Samantha," asked Sydney.

"Uh, Myra, went upstairs. But something is wrong with Samantha. She said she wanted to be alone, so she went down to the beach."

"Well, did she say anything," asked Sydney.

"Well, no. Hey, Sis, we were all having a good time when I mentioned that Matthew was here. Suddenly, she shut down. I tried talking to her, but she asked to be left alone."

"Matthew? Huh, that is strange. Well, give her space. Wait. Daniel are you interested in Samantha?"

"Yes, Sis. I am very interested in her. I wanted to talk to Matthew to see what is up, but I am not sure that is the right move."

"Boy, listen, are you crazy? Look over there. That is Matthew's personal assistant. Does he look like a lady to you? Just let her work it out, whatever it is. But whatever you do, don't you dare approach Matthew about anything. For once, Daniel, listen to me. Just freshen up and go to dinner. Leave this matter alone. Whatever it is. Matthew is here. If necessary, I know he will address it. Just leave it alone." Daniel looked out the window at Samantha at the beach. "Okay, Sis, I am going to trust you on this, but I really like her and I wanted to connect with her before she leaves in the morning."

"Daniel, if she is interested in you, do not worry she will let you know. I know you have already told her that you were interested in her, right?"

"Yeah, you know it. I had to jump on that right away."

"Well, whatever. Just do not talk to Matthew about Samantha, and let her have her space. I will see you at dinner."

"All right, Sis, see you soon." Daniel watched Matthew from the window as he approached Samantha on the beach. Daniel ran and stood quietly watching from the deck.

“Hello, Samantha.”
“Hello, Matt. Huh, I mean, Matthew.”
“Samantha, there is no easy way for me to say this, but your presence here this week is most disturbing for me. Did you intentionally contact my wife after what you put her or us through? It is unacceptable for you to be here. What is next? What have you planned next?”
“Matthew, I really hate you. I mean, really hate you. At one time, it really consumed me. For days all I could think about was getting back at you and your precious Becky. I told myself when Myra asked me to come. That I was coming because all of us in college made a vow to be girlfriends forever. Girlfriends forever, so much for making vows. What I really wanted to do was stick it to you one more time. I knew the minute you found out that I was here, you would stop at nothing to come rescue your precious little Becky. Matthew, you want to know what is next. I will tell you what is next? This trip has helped me to realize, I do not want to ever have anything to do with you or Rebecca, again, in life. Yes, I should have moved on by now. And yes, it is my fault that I am still hurt. But Matthew, I know you will never understand that being hurt by both the people you love and who you trusted to be your friends, well, it leaves a person with a deeper wound than they ever would imagine.
“What’s next Matthew?” said Samantha.
“Well, Matthew, you or Rebecca will never have to worry about me ever intentionally being in your life. I have decided as of right now to move on. You have a nice life.” Samantha walked back to the beach house.

“Samantha, wait a minute, asked Mark. “Listen, I am, again sorry that I or Rebecca hurt you. It was never my intentions to do so. I am sorry our friendship ended so badly. But Samantha, it was only a friendship and never anything more. Yes, I am glad that you have moved on. I, too, wish you God’s grace and His blessings upon your life.”

Samantha stared at Matthew and turned and walked away.

As Rebecca approached, she asked, “Honey, is everything okay?”

“Yes, yes. Everything is okay. We were just talking and finally able to make peace about the past. How are you dear?”

“I am fine Matthew. How is Samantha?”

“Uh, she is still very hurt, honey.”

“Well, Matthew, we will keep praying for her that she finds God’s peace, so he can heal her broken heart. Let us pray, honey, now.”

“Okay Becky,” Said Matthew.

Samantha returned to the beach house. “Who are you calling and what are you doing Samantha?”

“Girl, Myra, I got to get out of here. I should have never come. I have been such a fool to carry a torch for a man all these years, and who has never loved me. What on earth am I doing here? I called an Uber, and I am going to a hotel for tonight and catch my flight out in the morning.”

“Hey, I’m sorry. Do you want me to go with you?”

“No, I need to be alone. I have wasted ten years of my life. It is time for a sister to move on. I love you, Myra, but I need the time alone. I have truly been sitting in the dark and this trip made a light bulb come on."

"Are you sure you are all right?"

"Yeah, girl, don't worry. This is the best I have been in a long time. You know, seeing Matthew again, Myra brought back so much hate. I hated him. But what I see, is that it was all a waste of time. Hating him changed nothing, but it made me out to be a fool. Look at me, here. Crazy girl. Just think, I am wanting a man all these years who has never wanted me. Such a waste of time I will never get back. No, no, Myra, I got to move on. I do not know for the life of me why it took so long. I was just stuck and angry. Hey, say my goodbyes for me. My ride is here and I will see you in the morning on the plane."

"All right. Are you sure you do not want me to go with you?"

"Myra, look at me. I am sure. I am going to take a long bath. Funny, I may even take Matthew's advice," Samantha paused, "Maybe I will pray to God and ask for His peace." Samantha smiled and shook her head as she left out the door. "Bye girl."

"Have a good night. See you in the morning Sam."

Laughter filled the room, garnished with great food and all the stories of yesterday. "Well, Robert and Amanda, are you ready for twins," asked Belinda.

"Well, we do not know Sis. It doesn't matter, they are coming, so we got to be ready," laughed Robert.

"Hey, Myra, where have you been," asked Belinda.

"Seeing Samantha off. Samantha sends her goodbyes and she told me to tell you Sydney that she really appreciated you opening up your beach house to her."

"Oh, uh, why and when did she leave? Where did she go," asked Daniel.

"Uh, she wanted time alone. But do not worry she left you her number. Well, the food looks great. How is it?"

"Uh, all of it is good, Myra."

"Great what time is Liz coming back?"

"Who knows, said, Teddy. Maybe never," laughed Teddy.

Robert quickly looked at Teddy. "She should be back soon. I will stay up until she comes in, " said Robert.

"I know you will," laughed Teddy.

Everyone is laughing. "Hey when we finish let's go down to the beach and make a fire, and we will stay up until Liz comes home," laughed Sydney."

Six months later.

"Where is she at," asked Belinda. We have been planning this shower for weeks. "Rebecca, please go in the kitchen and check on Chef Rio, and see if the food is ready."

"Belinda, settle down. She will be here."

"I know, Myra, but I am so excited. Soon, my two nephews will be born."

"What's her due date, again?"

"First of next month."

"Two weeks," yelled Myra. "No wonder she is late. She is probably as big as a house."

"Myra, give her a break. I know it's hard for her to get around. Oh, oh, here she comes."

"Like I said, as big as a house. How many babies? Because she looks like she is carrying ten."

"Myra," yelled Sydney, "don't dare tell her that. When you are pregnant, you are very sensitive."
"Well, I would be sensitive too if I looked like that. How is she supposed to fit through the door?"
"Myra! Uh, okay."
"Liz, what took you guys so long?"
"Well, she had to go to the restroom about every two miles. So, we made ten stops along the way," laughed Liz.
"Where is Robert," asked Rebecca.
"He is on his way with the other guys."
"Here is my baby. How are you doing, girl? Ooh, you look so big, child. Are you sure there is only two babies in there," laughed Mrs. Peterson.
"Mom," yelled Belinda, "now you know that was not right."
"Child, I am just saying, how big can a woman get? I do not believe there is any more room in her stomach even to eat."
"Mom!"
"All right, I will let it alone. Amanda knows I love her and cannot wait for my two grandsons."
"Everyone is here. And now, as promised, Robert and I will reveal the names to you. Robert tell them the names."
"My oldest son, the first one who comes out will be named after daddy, Benjamin. And my youngest son will be named Theodore, also known as, Teddy."
Teddy jumped up and tackled Robert to the ground. Everyone erupted in laughter.
"Thank you, son, for the tribute. I am really touched Robert."

"You're welcome, daddy. I love you. Without you I would not be the man I am today. I wanted my sons to always remember that." The doorbell rang, "Go see who that is, Teddy."

"Hey it's Ethan."

Liz stood up. "Ethan? Uh, he told me he would be out of the country this week. Hey, what are you doing here?"

"What else, Liz? I am here for the shower." Liz looked strange. "What about your trip?"

"I had to cut it short. I had some important business to take care of and came home early."

"Oh, okay. Come on in and have a seat."

"Hey, dinner is ready," said Belinda.

Teddy stood up. "This toast is to my brother, Robert, and his lovely wife Amanda, who finally has a partner, so he can spend more time at home with his wife and his new babies. I pray that the Lord bless the birth of your sons. I also pray that he gives you more children."

"Hey, whoa! Let us have these, Teddy."

"I would like to pray a blessing for the babies, too."

"Okay, Ethan, the floor is all yours," laughed Teddy.

"May the Lord richly bless this family and the two wonderful new additions to it. May the Lord always be the center of your family's joy. And Elizabeth Irene Marshall, will you marry me?"

Silence filled the room. Every fork stopped and all eyes turned to Liz. Slowly Liz turned her head and stood. "Liz, you were the reason I cut my trip short. You are my important business. I wanted all of your family to be present when I asked you. Again, Elizabeth Irene Marshall will you marry me?"

Liz looked at Rebecca with tears in her eyes. "Uh, Ethan, uh, I will marry you."
The room exploded with joy!
"Oh, my goodness," shouted Belinda. "This is great! I am so happy Liz and Ethan!"
"Congratulations man and welcome to the family."
"Yeah, man, welcome aboard."
"Thanks Robert and Teddy."
"Wait. What is going on? Where are you ladies taking her?"
"You don't worry about Liz, Ethan, we have her now," said Rebecca.
"Well, you have done it now, boy. You can forget it. Those ladies have Liz, and you will not get her back until the wedding, so, get use to this. Just sit down here with the fellas and chill out."
"Yeah, man. Pops is right. It's all over now."
"Yeah, they will be pretty glued to each other until you walk Liz down the aisle. Come on and sit down man," laughed Robert.

The ladies go outside. Rebecca grabbed Liz close and they talk. "I am so happy for you Liz. I wanted you to experience love again. I know you shied away from it because you were afraid of being hurt. But I know that is not the will of the Lord for our lives. God never wanted our lives to be directed by fear, sorrow, and pain. He is such a loving God, too.

Always wanting us to experience the very best for our lives. Liz, the Lord would never allow you to shy away from loving someone because you were hurt the first time. I know because he allowed me, but God wants to become our enough. That no matter who is in or not in and out of our lives, as long as He is there, it is enough. He is all we need or desire. Yes, I prayed that you would find that resting place in God. And I got the joy of seeing God answer my prayers. Liz, I watched as God became your enough."

"Thank you, Rebecca. Thank you for praying for me all those years. Truly, I could not have survived without them. As I look back Rebecca, I am so grateful to have had you as my friend. I am so grateful that you did not give up on me. Yes, right now I am happy, and I truly do love Ethan. But I am so glad that God is my enough, and that He was my enough first. I am so thankful that God has satisfied my life."

"Yes, Liz, even as a married woman you will see God will remain your enough because He is still truly my enough."

Liz's special day arrived. "Dearly beloved, we are gathered here together in the sight of God and this company." As Pastor Carlton's words filled the church, all were present in much joy. Liz smiled as she thinks about the blessings of God bestowed upon her and her family. Again, Liz, knew everything was all right. She and Ethan are getting married with her best friend by her side, Rebecca, and Matthew and their boys. Sydney is also present with her kids and with her fiancé. Teddy is all smiles with his glowing pregnant wife, Sharon, and their boys. Robert and Amanda are so happy with their two beautiful baby boys, and Mark and Belinda, who is Liz's, voice of reason. Liz looked at her family and friends, and she thought to herself as she declared out loud, "And on this very day, "I, Elizabeth

Irene Marshall take Ethan Grayson, III, to be my husband. To have and hold until death do us part." Liz heard Pastor Carlton say, "Let us pray." She bowed her head and closed her eyes as tears streamed down her face. Her lips quivered as she whispered, "God, You have heard my cry. You have healed my heart and made me whole. I know you love me, and now we are your family. You are God all by yourself and you are a good God. Amen."

To order books send an email to:
sogalr2020@gmail.com
https://www.amazon.com/author/elviracraig

Other books by Elvira Craig

eBooks

soG, Abba's Love Reveal

...And I want a House with a White Picket Fence

Yes, He Is Enough

(The sequel to...And I Want A House with a White Picket Fence)

Paperbacks

Speaking the Father's Language

Been There, Done That

Unveiling the Things to Come

Marriage...Life, Love & Laughter

Marriage...Hot & Spicy Style

Empowerment Manual for Spiritual Warfare

Prophets and Their Prophetic Ministry

No, God is Not Mad at You

**Release soon*

The Kingdom Valuation*

Hidden Riches & Supernatural Beings*

About the Author

Elvira Craig accepted Jesu as a teenager. She grew up in Ford Heights and Beacon Hill, Illinois and holds a Bachelor's Degree in Psychology from Governors State University in Park Forest, Illinois.

As a young lady, Elvira traveled and ministered the Gospel; then God sent her to fellowship with Messianic Jews. Today, called as a minister of God, Elvira understands the reason she needed to know Israel: it is for the last days. God has called her to sound the alarm of His coming and has imparted to her revelation knowledge concerning the End Time Events. Elvira and her husband, Pastor Carlton Craig, are parents of three beautiful daughters/sons-in-law, and they are the grandparents to four fun-loving grandchildren. The Craigs are the Founders and Publishers of End Times Harvest Publication Ministries, a Biblical publication of teaching and evangelism. Today, Carlton and Elvira are the Pastors of Bible Teaching Fellowship Ministries in Spring and Lufkin, Texas. The Craigs are Overseers of Beth United Congregations (BUC)-located in California, Texas, and Kansas. The Craig's are also the hosts of the National Builder's Prayer under Mary Colbert. The Craig's are the founders of the Voices for the Voiceless, a prayer and action ministry in the protection of the unborn/children. Elvira is the founder of the Talk and Tell (TAT) an organization in the protection of children against sexual abuse and bullying. Pastor Elvira is the 17th Advisory Member of the Advisory Branch of The Joshua Generation (TJG). Under the leadership of Dr. Jose V. Pascua, Founder/President. Elvira is one of the 24 Elders of the

Worldwide Modern Online Christian Youth Business Consortium Network Movement.

www.ingramcontent.com/pod-product-compliance
Lightning Source LLC
LaVergne TN
LVHW051056080426
835508LV00019B/1900

9781891680380